Henry David Thoreau:
Studies and Commentaries

Henry David Thoreau:
Studies and Commentaries

Edited by
Walter Harding, George Brenner,
and Paul A. Doyle

Rutherford • Madison • Teaneck
Fairleigh Dickinson University Press

© 1972 by Associated University Presses, Inc.
Library of Congress Catalogue Card Number: 73-169815

Associated University Presses, Inc.
Cranbury, New Jersey 08512

First Printing February, 1972
Second Printing July, 1973

ISBN: 0-8386-1028-5
Printed in the United States of America

Contents

Foreword	7
Preface	11
Note	13
In Wildness Is Thoreau, by Lewis Leary	17
Thoreau's Concord, by Ruth Wheeler	25
Writing in the Dark, by Alfred Kazin	34
Thoreau, Charles Ives, and Contemporary Music, by Philip Corner	53
Panel Discussion on Thoreau, by Walter Harding, Donald Harrington, and Frederick T. McGill, Jr.	82
Thoreau and Poetry, by Muriel Rukeyser	103
Thoreau and India, by Kamala Bhatia	117
The Thoreau-Gandhi Syndrome, by Nissim Ezekiel	133
Thoreau's Influence on One Life, by George Russell Ready	144
Walking Westward, by Jack Schwartzman	150
About the Contributors	154

Foreword

In just a few short years the annual cultural festivals at Nassau Community College in Garden City, Long Island, have become a vibrant tradition, bringing the works and lives of some of our greatest American writers—Whitman, Emily Dickinson, and now Henry David Thoreau—into vividly meaningful focus not only for the thousands of young students on the Nassau Community College campus, but for the people of the whole county and much of the surrounding area.

As secretary of the Thoreau Society, it has been my pleasant duty to attend a great many meetings devoted to commemorating the life and works of Henry David Thoreau—annual meetings of the Thoreau Society itself in Concord, Massachusetts, and special meetings in points as widely varied as Detroit, Michigan; Logan, Utah; Paris, France; and Fukuoka, Japan. And at these meetings I have been constantly impressed with the impact that Henry David Thoreau is having a century after his death—an impact far greater than any he had on his own contemporaries. Thoreau speaks to our time. His works are far more alive, far more pertinent today than they were in his own day.

But there was a very special, a unique quality about the meetings held at Nassau Community College. As we sat there in the opening session in that auditorium converted from what was once a huge hangar for Mitchell Field, with the sunshine pouring in on a veritable sea of young faces—though the scene was a striking contrast with the quiet solitude of a cabin on the shores of Walden Pond—there was a feeling of intense intellectual excitement in the air, with the students suddenly discovering that here in Thoreau was a voice out of the past that really spoke to them. A college generation that liked to boast that they trusted no one over thirty suddenly discovered that someone born one hundred and fifty years ago could be meaningful to them.

This, fortunately, was no staid gathering of scholarly pedants who were interested merely in footnoting and comma-correcting. The festival committee had chosen their speakers well; they chose men and women who were excited by Thoreau's meaningfulness. And their excitement was contagious to their audience. Most of the papers collected herein are transcriptions made from tapings of the actual speeches, many of which were to a large extent extemporaneous. As a result the word-choice and composition are, on occasion, more colloquial than usual, and a few quotations may possibly not be exact. But the resulting informality, I believe, gives a sense of presence at these meetings that is rarely captured in such a volume. The ideas and the meetings come alive herein.

One essay, that by Philip Corner, will undoubtedly puzzle, perhaps even outrage some readers, both by its content and by its method of presentation. To me at least, the reproduction of this manuscript catches some of the spirit of the essay. And as to the content, I will only remind you that Thoreau prefaced his masterpiece with the epigraph, "I do not propose to write an ode to dejection, but to brag as lustily as chanticleer in the morning, standing on his roost, if only to wake the neighbors up."

If there seems to be a special emphasis in the volume on Thoreau and the Orient, remember that Lin Yutang once called Thoreau the "most Oriental" of American authors. Not only did he derive a great part of his inspiration from the East, but his own impact on the East has been greater than that of any other American writer.

I was not surprised a few weeks ago to run across the statement in an issue of a popular magazine to the effect that in the long run Henry David Thoreau will have proved to be the greatest influence on the twentieth century—more so than that of Einstein or Freud or Marx or Hitler. One should emerge from a reading of this volume with an appreciation of the validity of that statement.

Walter Harding, Secretary
The Thoreau Society
State University of New York: Geneseo

Preface

A few years ago, the Nassau College English Department conceived the idea of having an annual cultural festival honoring famous American writers. Not only would the English Department participate, but the Art, Music, Theatre, Library, and Speech units of the college were also to be involved in the celebration. Accordingly, the first of the Festivals—the one honoring Walt Whitman—was arranged. Among the participants were Robert Penn Warren, Gay Wilson Allen, Sculley Bradley, Malcolm Cowley, Muriel Rukeyser, William Meredith, W. D. Snodgrass, Babette Deutsch, Karl Shapiro, and John Ciardi. The college commissioned Paul Shyre to write an original drama for the occasion, and this project resulted in *A Whitman Portrait,* starring James Whitmore and Barbara Barrie. This play was later produced Off-Broadway and has subsequently been performed by a touring company at many colleges in California and in the Middle West. The eminent bibliophile Charles E. Feinberg loaned first editions and manuscript material for the concomitant library display. Mr. Feinberg also exhibited the now classic letter written by Ralph Waldo Emerson to Walt Whitman on July 21, 1855, congratulating Whitman at the beginning of a great career. Among the libraries and institutions which sent materials were the University of Texas, the Library of Congress, Duke University, and the University of Pennsylvania.

From this origin have grown the subsequent literary

festivals at Nassau Community College. Famous figures continued to appear, and they offered satisfying intellectual and aesthetic experiences. Richard Wilbur, Denise Levertov, Julie Harris, Robert Ryan, Kim Hunter, Richard Sewall, Anne Sexton—these are just a few of the important names gracing the later celebrations. The art exhibits, choral groups, orchestra productions, original plays, and almost comprehensive library exhibits continued to increase in quality and elaborateness so that, for example, at the Thoreau Festival, the Buffalo Philharmonic Orchestra traveled to Long Island and performed with the aid of a grant from the Rockefeller Foundation.

The Thoreau Festival was particularly well received. Again, for instance, the library display was exceptional. The core of the exhibit was loaned by the eminent Thoreauvian collector Leonard F. Kleinfeld, who shared his valuable editions and albums with a large and appreciative audience. The Pierpont Morgan Library, Mrs. Millicent Todd Bingham—who did so much to make the Emily Dickinson Festival a delight, Southern Illinois University Library, and the Archives of the Thoreau Lyceum also participated in the bibliophile aspect of the program.

But most of all, and rightly so, the speakers and those scholars who participated in the panel discussion drew the principal attention. Because so many of their comments and thoughts were perceptive and deeply meaningful, it was decided to record these materials on a more permanent basis, especially since Thoreau and his works seem to grow more and more important and become more widely publicized with each passing moment. That he has now been adopted by the hippies and that his "Civil Disobedience" essay is presently in everyone's mind are just two of the many manifestations of the contemporaneity of his ideas and of his significance as one of America's greatest writers and most stimulating thinkers. To count-

less pre-hippie Americans, *Walden* is still a vade mecum
to which one turns for solace and inspiration amid the
turbulence of twentieth-century existence. In the light of
these facts, we believe that the writers whose work appears
in this *Festschrift* deserve a close reading because they
stimulate thought about, and bring an increase of knowledge of, a man whose "soul," as Emerson remarked, "was
made for the noblest society."

George Brenner
P. A. Doyle

Nassau Community College
State University of New York
Garden City, Long Island

NOTE

The essay by Alfred Kazin has been copyrighted by
him and may not be reprinted elsewhere without his
written permission.

Muriel Rukeyser's "Thoreau and Poetry" is copyrighted
by her and may not be reprinted without her written
permission.

All the essays, speeches, and discussions herein are
printed with the permission of their respective authors.

Mr. Corner's music manuscript was given by him to
the Fales Collection, New York University. It has been
furnished to the editors of this book through the courtesy
of the Special Collections Library of New York University.

Henry David Thoreau:
Studies and Commentaries

In Wildness Is Thoreau

Lewis Leary

I WOULD HAVE US THINK BRIEFLY ABOUT THE THOREAU WHO was a wild man, who let his hair grow long, and finally grew a beard, who dressed as he wished, and did exactly what he wished. He thought that many of his Concord neighbors led "mean and sneaking" lives, going around desperately in circles, so caught within convention that they were confused and bewildered. But not Henry Thoreau! "My brave Henry," Emerson called him; he believed in himself; he was confident that what he thought to be right was right, and he cared not at all whether other people agreed with him or not. He was, that is to say, a supreme and impossible egoist. Literally, said Emerson, he was "the most child-like, unconscious, and unblushing egoist it has been my fortune"—note with what characteristic carefulness Emerson chooses his words ("fortune," not "misfortune")—"to encounter."

But to some people Thoreau was something of a bore, who talked too much and studied too diligently to be different. Hawthorne thought him an "intolerable bore, who was the exception to every rule, the judge of all the rest of the universe." In talking, he droned on and on, "monotonously didactic, deliberately obscure, playing with words, puns." His name, he might say, was Henry Thoreau, with accent on the first syllable; I am a thorough man: I do things thoroughly; I see thoroughly.

17

To some people, especially of our generation, he seems simply sick, a maimed man, home-centered, with a domineering mother whom he could not, and was not sure whether he really wanted to, escape. New York frightened him, and the mountains of Maine frightened him. He preferred, he said, to sit inconspicuously at the back door of Concord, and mostly alone. And it has been suggested that his sexual life was neither as whole nor as wholesome as it might have been. So, lacking this and lacking that, unequipped to meet the world on *its* terms, he made a kind of separate peace with living, secretly wishing, secretly courting, failure. "I rarely look people in their faces," he once admitted.

He *was* a strange man, and strange stories have been collected about him, but the point to be made is that this strange man is dead and may perhaps just as well be forgotten—as a man, that is, who is to be admired and imitated. Hawthorne found him in person an incredible bore, and I discover myself among those who find him also a bore in the tales which people tell about him and the quirky things he did. He was "an intolerable bore," Hawthorne attested, but then Hawthorne went on to say, he was a *good* writer. And it is this writer—this *good* writer—whom I hope we celebrate today, the artist who was tough, and witty, and stoic, and wild! Not the man who was crotchety, even perhaps a little vulgar.

"A revolutionary of absolute faith," he has been called, who started a one-man revolution which has overturned worlds—but not through what he did, only through what he wrote. He wrote of disobedience, of saying No, of resisting passively, of doing only what in the best sense comes naturally, thus leaving us, in the words of Martin Luther King, "an inestimable legacy of creative protest." "I would remind my countrymen"—everyone today recognizes these words—that they are to be "men first and Americans only at a late or convenient hour." And then he asks, "How does it become a man to act toward this American government today? In Thoreau's eyes, no man of sane sense could "without disgrace be associated with it." He was wild indeed when he advises, "If the law requires you to be an agent of injustice, I say to you break that law." The law will never make men free; it's men who must make law free. This is subversive, in the wildest and truest sense. It is anarchic. If everyone acted as Thoreau acted, or did as he advised, what would happen? Who would keep the store or man the guns? It seems patently preposterous! But try it, Thoreau advised; try it and see!

Now that is pert, and it is perky, and it is provocative, just as Thoreau meant it to be. But perhaps he is putting us on. There's a little of humbug in every successful writer, because, as we remember, Thoreau was not, in fact, an activist at all—except briefly in crisis, when he forgot to be an individual and broke laws cooperatively with other people in helping man a station on the underground railroad, which may prove that Thoreau was not *just* a writer, but was willing to stand up and be counted, as we say, when there was something worth being counted for. But mainly he was a writer and a joyous humbug, who played with reader and with words. When he spoke of raising beans beside Walden Pond, he spoke in proper Concord dialect of *beings* also; he raised *beings*. His sit-in at Walden was for purpose beyond eccentric show. He went there to write books which might raise beings, and, the books being written, he left.

Don't go ripping seams trying to put on my coat if it doesn't fit you, he tells his neighbors: this is my way of finding time to do what I want to do, of cutting off irrelevancies. Have the niceness to find your own way; keep your own eyes open; look about you: "Only that day dawns to which you are awake." That is what *Walden* is about. It is about keeping awake, noticing things, seeing

things, and with your own eyes only. Take off the blinders
that family or school or society has tied about your eyes.
Who is it that makes you think what you think you
think? Have you ever had a thought? Have you ever
really seen something for yourself, seeing it as it is and
not what other people have told you that it is. For your
own sake, and for the saving of the world, Thoreau pleads,
do wake up! Stop leading "lives of quiet desperation,"
for there is "more day to dawn. The sun is but a morning
star."

Now that is patent nonsense. The sun is not a morning
star; the sun is a sun is a sun. Thoreau plays with words
as he plays with readers, creating in prose a poetry which
is elusive and wild. "In wildness," he said, "is the preservation of the world." He wished to speak a word for
absolute freedom and wildness, freedom to regard man
as an inhabitant of nature rather than as a member of
society. As a man, that is, rather than as an American, a
Concordian, a member of the Thoreau Society, or a Negro,
or a Vietnamese. Give me wildness, he asked, "whose
glance no civilization can endure," for life consists in wildness. Dullness is just another word for tameness. The
most alive is the wildest. Stop trying to be good, he said,
and start trying to be good for something. That is pert
and witty, and Thoreau as a writer is pert and witty, and
wild and eccentric.

He avoids beaten tracks, for truth, he has said, is wild
and shy, and hard to come on. Truth is elusive. Its meaning is to be captured only with great difficulty, after great
care. It must often be approached indirectly, as an elusive
wild thing must be approached. Humor can snare truth
often more securely than seriousness can, and puns can
insinuate truth, and absurdities often can also. Sobriety
comes with civilization, and with fear. Thoreau was
serious enough and wild enough to play with words, and
with humor, and the comic scene in which man can play

a vigorous part, if he would only have the niceness to stay awake. Thoreau sings no song of doom, but of wildness that is alert to possibilities which each new dawn may reveal.

And because as a writer he is gay and witty and evasive, Thoreau is often difficult to read, and even more difficult to understand. He sometimes, as E. B. White has said, packs his sentences so full of meanings that they are one hundred percent anchovy—so rich that taken too many at a time they can bring about a kind of mental indigestion.

Thoreau wove a basket, he explained, which was "intricately designed," and in which he would catch and keep truth for all men to see. An impossible task this, if taken seriously, as if truth could be caught and kept! But people who take Thoreau seriously are often caught, and immediately and intensely, in one or another of the traps which he has set. They believe what this man Thoreau has said, and thus allow him to make up their minds for them, rather than thinking, seeing, understanding, for themselves. They follow in Thoreau's footsteps, rather than make tracks of their own.

In fact, if Thoreau had his way completely, we might spend little time in reading him: "Read the best books first," he advised, and though he, being human, must have hoped that his were among those best books, he was not ever quite sure. He named some of those books which he did think best, which he called the "bibles of mankind," the sacred books of the East, some of the classics of Greece and Rome, Chaucer and Shakespeare, and a few besides. Read these first, Thoreau advises, or you may never have a chance to read them.

Certainly, he went on, we need not, in what we read or think, be soothed and entertained always, like children. Thoreau agreed with his neighbor Emerson that the function of literature was not to soothe or entertain. Emerson had clearly said that a writer, when he is worth reading, does not try to settle anything; his function is to unsettle all things. He who resorts to an easy novel because he is languid, said Thoreau, does no better than if he took a nap—or, we might add, an aspirin or a martini. For Thoreau asks us to prefer books that are wild, which dare beyond what is conventional and safe and soothing: books which afford us, not a cowering enjoyment, but in which each thought is of unusual daring, such as an idle man cannot read and a timid man would not be entertained by. Books like these—and his—can make us dangerous to institutions.

To be wild, to be dangerous to institutions, to disobey what one cannot in conscience approve, to simplify, to see and act for ourselves—to such as these Thoreau invites us wildly, wittily, evasively. But finally the measure of our reliance on him is our reliance on ourselves. If we say, Yes, this that Thoreau says or suggests is right, and that therefore we are going to do exactly what he says or suggests because he certainly does see the situation as it exists, then we are misreading Thoreau. We are caught up. We are taken in. We become victims of his wild humbuggery. If, because Thoreau went to jail rather than obey a law which he could not approve, we say (for just one example) that we should go to jail for the same reason—if we say this, we are using his mind, we are using his perceptions, and not our own. Only that day breaks to which *we* are awake.

What Thoreau thought is really not so important as the fact that he thought. That he was a writer, a person who saw clearly in the circumstance in which he found himself—that *is* important. When Martin Luther King spoke of Thoreau's legacy of protest, he called it, you recall, a legacy of "creative protest," not imitative protest. Thoreau imitated no one, not even himself. He called for creation, not creed; for fellow explorers, not placid followers.

Thoreau was an artist, not a thinker; he was a see-er, not a seer. And those who take his thought too seriously are not thinkers either, certainly not see-ers; they are simply imitators, disciples, smudged carbons. Wake up, Thoreau said, and that is virtually all that he said, and that is enough. Do it yourself. Get off my back. Live your own lives, not mine. He is wild, this Thoreau; and he is eccentric—off the beaten path. He nibbled his asparagus from the wrong end, said Oliver Wendell Holmes. He stood off from things to see them more closely. He came close to things to get a distant view. Maybe he did not see very well at all. The chances are that he was mostly wrong, as most people are mostly wrong.

He is elusive and egotistical, and he sometimes does talk too much, but he is alive and he invites response— not necessarily agreement, but response; and through response he means to shock us to wakefulness because we have slept too long, being civil, servile, and obedient. Whatever is it, he asked, that gets into people that makes them behave so docilely and so well? As an artist, Thoreau presented an artist's honest view of the world, and that is a very great distinction indeed. How dishonest of us, and how without distinction, when we accept his view as our own. Wake up! he commanded. Do your own seeing. Keep alert.

His own senses were almost always alive. He slept, someone has said, only at night in bed. If he was different from other men of his time, it was because he was thus constantly alert, and when he speaks to our time, he requires, not assent, not agreement or imitation, but answering liveliness, and some wildness also. For in this "wildness," in every sense of the world, is, he insisted, "the preservation of the world." Who wants a tame man? Or a tamed poet? Or a tamed Thoreau? There is no such thing unless, without eyes to see or mind to wonder, people read him so carelessly as to suppose that Thoreau wanted others to be doing what he did, rather than doing—as see-ers in their own right—what comes to them most naturally. Thoreau has outdared most of his readers in wildness. That may not be a good thing; but it is, I think, what he intended—not as program, but as challenge which has too often gone unanswered. An imitation Thoreau is neither wild nor wise.

Thoreau's Concord

Ruth Wheeler

DONALD CULROSS PEATTIE, WRITING IN THE *New York Times* back in 1940, said of Concord, "If a New Englander could point to but one town and say of it 'Thus we were', that town would surely be Concord, the cradle of plain living and high thinking. For the glory of Concord, preeminent among small towns, is the independent and upright spirit of the men who made it great. There was a little host of them: writers, poets, ministers—fearless and intractable abolitionists—but two stand out as immortals, men who did more to shape the philosophy of American daily life than any others who lived here or anywhere else. They were Ralph Waldo Emerson and Thoreau—Thoreau who by withdrawing from the world plumped his name and fame and thought squarely into the middle of it." This is the sort of article that little old ladies in Concord clip out and save. But, like a Concordian and a true disciple of Thoreau, I question it.

Concord, 100 or 150 years ago, was not solely writers, ministers, poets, or fearless and intractable abolitionists. Thoreau was the one writer who knew that, for he was a keen observer of human nature as well as of wild nature. "As I walked in the woods," he wrote, "to see the birds and squirrels, so I walked in the village to see the men and boys." If you look at the chapter headings in *Walden*, you will see that "Solitude" is followed by "Visitors"; "The

Bean-field" by "The Village"; and "Brute Neighbors" by
"House-warming," "Former Inhabitants; and Winter Visitors." Notice that word "Former." Thoreau usually read
the first version of his books to an audience of townspeople,
so that he could not describe too particularly the living
worthies of the village, since his sense of fitness differed
from that of our present-day "instant historians," our
Manchesters and junior Schlesingers.

One fact about these former inhabitants I should like
to stress. Zilpha White, whom we would tuck away and
forget in a mental institution, was allowed to live as she
pleased in her little cabin on the edge of Thoreau's bean-
field—what was later his beanfield—but she was not forgotten. The busy farmers' wives took her their wool and
flax to weave, and when she was too old to weave, the
Female Charitable Society (so their records say) took her
a bushel of corn, tea, sugar, rice, a hand of tobacco and
brandy—a rather interesting menu.

The Negroes, Brister and Fenda, were supported by a
legacy from their former master, Squire Cumings, who
had named the selectmen to administer it. With his basic
needs cared for, Brister circulated as a handyman through
the community. The feeble-minded in the poorhouse were
still a part of the community. They were taken care of
by their families as long as possible, and when they came
at last on the town were still a familiar sight on the streets.
When Ellen Emerson, aged ten, was visiting her uncle on
Staten Island, Thoreau wrote to tell her of the death of
poor crazy old William Brown in the poorhouse. He used
to beg for pennies. "Who will have his sense now?" said
Thoreau.

Thoreau's first printed article was an obituary notice
for Anna Jones, who had been a girl of twenty at the
time of the Revolution. Thoreau had been to see her in
the poorhouse, for the Concord battle at the bridge was

still a living reality. Thoreau also liked to get history firsthand from George Minott, whose father had been wounded at Bunker Hill. I like to think of Thoreau sitting on a wheelbarrow in George's sunny woodshed with a cat on his lap while George told about the good old days; not about large affairs, for George Minott had traveled the eighteen miles to Boston but once in his life—he'd never been on the railroad. But he knew where the old passenger pigeon roosts were, and where the turkey shoots were held, and was full of stories about the old traders, including John Beaton, whose widow had married George's grandfather.

Perhaps Thoreau had some fellow feeling for the Scottish trader, for he had a Scottish grandmother as well as a French grandfather to add to his two Yankee grandparents. It is a commonplace of agriculture that the cross-fertilization of different strains produces hybrids that differ from and may excel either parent. Many observers believe that the mingling of many different strains is the secret of American greatness. If this be so, may I suggest that Thoreau was perhaps our first truly American author.

Let us consider what Concord was like in Thoreau's formative years. A small town of 1500 people, it was too small to have strata. Few were poor and none was rich. Of about 850 male inhabitants, two-thirds were boys, and of the remaining men, all but about a hundred were farmers. The population before the Revolution had been as numerous. Families continued to be large, but every family lost at least half its boys to the frontier. "Their wagons rattled down the western hills," said Emerson, and the familiar Concord surnames could even then be found in every state and territory. Some historians have been unkind enough to say that all the originality and energy of the Puritan stock was thus drained away, but I prefer to think of the widened horizons of Concord homes where, through letters home or visits away, the Western Reserve or the Maine forests were familiar in every household.

Thoreau had cousins in Southern New Hampshire and in Jonesborough and Bangor, Maine.

Doubtless the man who, more than any other, stamped his character on Concord was Ezra Ripley, Minister of the First Parish from 1778 to 1841. He was the embodiment of old-time religion, with so strong a belief in a personal God that he even looked to Heaven to keep off the rain until his hay was under cover or, in time of drought, felt that his personal prayer for rain would be more effective than that of his young and inexperienced assistant.

An eminently practical man, he first came to Concord with his Harvard classmates in 1775 when the whole college moved to the country so that General Washington's army besieging Boston could take over the college buildings. The books were being moved out to Concord while the Battle of Bunker Hill was in progress.

When Concord's fiery young minister, Reverend William Emerson, enlisted as a chaplain in a local company and died in the service, Ezra Ripley succeeded him in the church and soon married the widow. She already had five children and after due intervals had three more. It was typical of Ezra Ripley that he paid the Emerson children for their share of the property so that he could leave the old manse to his own son, Samuel Ripley. Throughout his life he welcomed Emerson and Ripley children alike, and some of Ralph Waldo's happiest days were spent in the manse with his step-grandfather, who often took the boy with him when making parish calls, never failing to point out as they passed the house of some unfaithful parishioner that such as he had invariably come to a bad end.

This was the minister who baptized the infant Thoreau

and against whose interpretation of religion the young Thoreau rebelled.

Another familiar village figure was Nehemiah Ball, Town Clerk, Trial Justice, and Secretary of the School Committee. I suppose every town has such a willing worker who gets elected or appointed to every small-town job which no one else wants. A frequent debater at the Lyceum, he amused the irreverent boys by interjecting the phrase, "I apprehend," into every sentence. I apprehend that every speaker has such a mannerism. "In my judgment," is heard in every second sentence of the New York junior Senator's speeches. Nehemiah Ball introduced the Lyceum to the magic lantern. Throwing on a sheet the picture of a lion, he could think of no comment except, "This, I apprehend, is a ferocious beast." As a judge he took every difficult case under advisement. His biographer says of him, "He was cold, calculating and cautious; precise, prosey and pompous," while some of his friends considered him "deliberate, dignified and devout." Twenty years older than Thoreau, he hired that young man just out of Harvard in 1837 to teach the village school. It was he who visited school and ordered the young teacher to use the strap more liberally. Apparently the debate about proper education largely consisted, in those days, of a discussion as to whether the razor strop, the birch, or the ferrule was more effective. You remember that Thoreau obeyed, whipping several pupils for no discernible reason, then writing out his resignation, saying in a letter that he had always considered leather a nonconductor; unlike the electric wire, not a single spark of truth is ever transmitted through its agency.

This was the first example of several attempts in his lifetime to demonstrate his beliefs by a fitting practical example. As you will remember, he went to jail for one night to protest the Mexican War and its aftermath of new slave states, and went to Walden for two years to reduce life to its bare essentials. In no case did he consider it necessary to continue these demonstrations any longer than he needed to make his point, an example which I should like to recommend to present-day protesters.

Just as Ezra Ripley embodied religion and Nehemiah Ball embodied the accepted education of that day, so Samuel Staples embodied the shrewd and practical self-made man, admired for his industry and shrewdness.

The Middlesex Hotel fronted the green while the jail was conveniently behind it, so that the prisoners could be fed from the hotel kitchen. The sheriff's house was beside the hotel. Samuel Staples was successively stable boy, bartender and assistant to the sheriff, finally sheriff, charged with locking up the prisoners every night and getting them to court next day. During the day the prisoners, except those incarcerated for capital crimes, were allowed to ramble around the block within the jail limits and could enjoy Johnny Wesson's fiddle music in the evening as the hotel-keeper's son sat on the back steps to play.

Sam Staples soon married Lucinda, Johnny's sister, but so bitter were the Wessons against the local ministers for their temperance sermons that Sam and Lucinda had to make do with a retired minister from down the Boston Road, Ralph Waldo Emerson, who brought along two dinner guests as witnesses. They were Bronson Alcott and John S. Dwight, an unusual wedding party chosen for an unusual reason.

After the railroad was built, there was a greatly increased demand for wood which could be sold to the railroad or shipped to Boston. Vague boundaries of pine stumps or marked oak trees were not enough when wood was worth cash, so that there was more work for a good surveyor. The accommodating Staples often carried the

chain for Thoreau, and they liked each other in spite of
what each considered the other's peculiarities.

Wesson and Staples bought a tract of land opposite
the hotel, cut a road through, and laid it out in lots.
Thinking that the lot nearest the square was a fine place
for a church, and feeling as he did about the temperance
sentiments of the two old churches, Staples put up a sign
in the tavern one day reading, "All those in favor of
universal salvation meet here on Friday evening." They
met and organized a Universalist Church and hired a
preacher for five hundred dollars a year, but he proved a
disappointment, soon backsliding—if that is the word—into
temperance. "For a salary as small as that, I can afford to
be honest," he said. But as a consequence, the tavern-
keeper withdrew his support, the religious society died,
and before long the empty church was bought for the
new Catholic population.

Temperance had other victims. Dr. Bartlett was attend-
ing a temperance meeting one evening when Timothy
Prescott said it was all very well for Dr. Bartlett to try
to deprive others of the solace of alcohol, while himself
deriving solace from the pernicious habit of tobacco.
Bartlett rose, walked over to the stove, and threw in the
plug of tobacco he was chewing. "If my habit encourages
anyone to drink, so help me, I will never chew again."
He never did, though his daughters said that he paced
the floor for several nights afterward to calm his nerves
while trying to break the habit.

Living only a few doors from the tavern, the Doctor
was sometimes the victim of vandalism as the regulars
walked home after a convivial evening, throwing acid
through the parlor window, girdling the apple trees, shav-
ing the horse's tail, and once cutting the chaise top to
ribbons. The Doctor never had the carriage repaired,
driving it with the tatters streaming until the perpetrators
were shamed.

This was Thoreau's family doctor. He attended Thoreau's lectures, including the memorial to John Brown. He sent his girls to the Thoreau brothers' school, and Martha, the oldest daughter, is said to have had a broken heart when John Thoreau died. She never married.

I will leave it to others to tell of Emerson's influence on Thoreau, or Thoreau's on Emerson, to psychoanalyze Thoreau *ex post facto* as seems to be the style nowadays. Others can tell of the stimulus of Bronson Alcott's philosophic reflections, or of William Ellery Channing's aesthetics. No one has the skill to exactly assess the effect of background on a genius. But I believe, or perhaps I should say, "in my judgment" the truly great periods of culture the world over had their backgrounds in villages so small that all types were known to each other. Athens was a small city where the artisans were side by side with the scholars in the stoa. Florence, in Dante's day, was a small city where all kinds of people prepared for heaven or hell. The London of Shakespeare's day had cutthroats and Doll Tearsheets as well as great ladies and courtiers. Weimar was a small town as Goethe and Schiller knew it. All were small enough so that all the inhabitants were known to each other. I have yet to see a great writer emerge from a group of people of similar tastes and background, whether it be Greenwich Village, the editorial rooms of the *New Yorker*, or even a college professors' cocktail party. How are you going to see life steadily and see it whole if your contacts are largely with like-minded people? The human mind probably needs the encouragement of like minds; but more than that, it needs the testing and dialogue of a variety of different people, such as Thoreau found in Concord Village.

Thoreau was lucky to have been born in such a village. He was not a product of the working class, though he worked for a living. There were, it might be argued, no classes in Concord. He was not a product of a small group of intellectuals, although there was such a group, and their exchange of ideas was important to him. He knew all the village eccentrics. He was one, though he was not like any of them. He was the product of a varied ancestry, and a varied background. He was sui generis—his own man.

Writing in the Dark

Alfred Kazin

IN THE MORGAN LIBRARY IN NEW YORK ONE CAN SEE THE box that Thoreau built to hold his journals. This work runs to thirty-nine manuscript volumes and fourteen published volumes. It contains nearly two million words, more than 7000 printed pages. I do not know if it is the longest journal ever kept; probably not, for Thoreau, who kept it assiduously from the time he was twenty, died before he was forty-five, probably of the struggle I am about to describe. But of one thing about this journal I am sure; it is one of the most fanatical, most arduous, most tragic examples in history of a man trying to live his life by writing it—of a man seeking to shape his life, to *make* it, by words, as if words alone would not merely report his life but become his life by the fiercest control that language can exert.

The greatest part of Thoreau's life was writing, and this is probably true of many writers, especially in our time, when so many writers are interested not merely in composing certain books but in making a career out of literature. But what makes Thoreau's case so singular, and gives such an unnatural severity to his journal itself, is that the work of art he was seeking to create was really himself—his life was the explicit existence that he tried to make out of words. The act of writing became for him

not a withdrawal from life, a compensation for life, a
higher form of life—all of which it has been for so many
writers since Romanticism identified the act of composition with personal salvation. It became a symbolic form
of living, a way of living, *his* way of living. Writing was
this close to living, parallel to living, you might say,
because the only subject of Thoreau's life was himself.
He transcribed his life directly onto paper—by which I do
not mean that he reported it actually, but that he sought
to capture experience in just one form: the sensations
and thoughts of a man walking about all day long. To
this commonplace daily round he was restricted by his
own literal experience, for he did not wish in the slightest
to invent anything and was incapable of doing so. But he
was also restricted by the fact that he had no experience
to report except being a writer and looking for topics.
Thoreau never married. Wherever possible, as one can
tell from his most famous book, he lived alone; but since
this was in fact not always possible, for many members
of his family kept together by not marrying and also had
the family's pencil business to keep them together, he
went about alone and became a naturalist in his own
idiosyncratic style, an observer who could find material on
every hillside, a "self-appointed inspector of snow-storms
and rain-storms." He had his favorite classics to quote
from in his journal, books that he used as quotations
because they were of the greatest practical use to him;
he had this large family, full of eccentrics like himself
whom he needed to get away from, and he had a few
friends—associates of his ideas rather than intimate friends
—notably his employer and sometime patron, Emerson,
with whom his journal records the endless friction that
was so necessary in his relation with even the most for-
bearing individualists in New England. Otherwise Thoreau
might have felt that he was betraying his ideal life, the
life that nobody would conceive for himself but himself,

that he lived only in the epiphanies of his journal, that nobody could live except with himself alone.

Since books were really personal instruments, and friends were invariably, sooner or later, to betray his design for life, this left for subject matter, in a book of two million words, what one might call the American God, the only God left to these wholly self-dependent transcendentalists in the New England of the 1840s—Nature. Thoreau told Moncure Conway that he found in Emerson "a world where truths existed with the same perfection as the objects he studied in external nature, his ideals real and exact." Nature, by which Emerson meant everything outside the writer for him to explore and to describe—Nature for Thoreau became the landscape, mostly around Concord, that he could always walk into. It served as the daily occasion of Thoreau's journal, the matter that tied Thoreau to the world outside, that became the world, and that safely gave him something to write about each day. Nature gave him the outside jobs he took as a surveyor from time to time to get some money and to keep him in some practical relation to his town and his neighbors. Nature even made him a "naturalist," a collector of specimens and Indian relics, a student of the weather and of every minute change in the hillsides that he came to know with the familiarity that another man might have felt about the body of his wife.

But above all Nature was himself revealed in Nature, it was the great permissiveness in which he found himself every day. Nature was perfect freedom, Nature was constant health and interest, Nature was the perfection of visible existence, the ideal friend, the perfect because always predictable experience—it was ease and hope and thought such as no family, and certainly no woman, would ever provide. Nature was God, because God to Thoreau meant not the Totally Other, what is most unlike us—but perfect satisfaction.

That is what God had begun to mean to Emerson and other proud evangels of the new romantic faith that God lives *in* us and *as* us—that God is manifested by the power and trust we feel ourselves. Emerson was the oracle of a faith that only he could fully understand, because it rested on his gift for finding God in and through himself. Emerson's faith was pure inspiration; without his presence to give testimony, the intuition's access to the higher mysteries, or what Coleridge had called "reason," had to be painfully approximated by secondary faculties like the "understanding." Emerson was thus the unique case among modern writers of a spiritual genius whose role was essentially public, such as the founders of religion have played. Without his incomparable face, his living voice, Emerson on the printed page was never to inspire in later generations what the magnetism of his presence had created in his own day—a grateful sense on the part of many of his auditors that here was the founder, the oracle, the teacher of his tribe. Emerson, a very gifted writer, was first of all the appointed leader who comes in at the beginning, sounds a new hope and purpose, out of himself passes spiritual strength to the people.

Thoreau's life was entirely private and was lived, you might say, for himself alone. Except for his explosive political concern about the growing power of the slave interest, which was getting such an influence over the United States government that Thoreau properly discerned in it a threat to *his* absolute freedom as well as an affront to his wholly personal Christianity, he was, of course, not merely indifferent to the State but contemptuous of it. He was interested in "society" only as an anthropologist of sorts taking notes on his Concord neighbors and their peculiar ways. His God was private to himself and really not to be taught to, or shared with, anyone else. You might say it was imaginative pure power, Henry Thoreau's most perfection acquisition, in a narrow life that sought only a few acquisitions, and these the brightest and purest—pure morality, pure love, pure creation in the pages of his journal he rewrote each night from the notes taken on his walks.

God was not a person; He was the meaning you caught in the woods as you passed. But of course other poets of nature were saying this in the first half of the nineteenth century in England, Germany, and the United States. What Thoreau was saying, in prose of exceptional vibration, was that he had this God, this immanence in the woods, for and to himself whenever he wanted to; that he had only to walk out every afternoon (having spent the morning rewriting his field notes for his formal journal), to walk into the woods, to sit on the cliffs and look out over the Concord River and Conantum hills, for the perfect satisfaction to return again. As late as 1857, he could write in his journal: ". . . cold and solitude are friends of mine . . . I come to my solitary woodland walk as the homesick go home. This stillness, solitude, wildness of nature is a kind of thoroughwort or boneset, to my intellect. This is what I go out to seek. It is as if I always met in those places some grand, serene, immortal, infinitely encouraging, though invisible companion, and walked with him."

The satisfaction lay first of all in the daily, easy access to revelation, for sauntering—a word which Thoreau playfully derived from à la sainte terre, to the holy land—his mind dreamily overran what he saw even when he was most assiduously playing the inspector of snowstorms and rainstorms, overran it and filled up the spaces with evidence of design, growth, meaning. If you constantly note the minute changes in plants and animals, you create the figure of Nature as a single organism with the irresistible tendency to explain herself to you. The visible surface of things then shines with the truth of the evolutionary moral that Emerson had so contentedly taken away from his visit to the Botanical Garden in Paris on July 13, 1833, of which he wrote—"Not a form so grotesque, so savage, nor so beautiful but is an expression of some property inherent in man the observer,—an occult relation between the very scorpions and man. I feel the centipede in me,—cayman, carp, eagle, and fox. I am moved by strange sympathies; I say continually 'I will be a naturalist.' " Thoreau's sympathies with the rough and the wild were so intense that he hauntingly identified himself with other forms of life, but they also dumbly and pleasingly arranged themselves to an eye that could not have been more unlike the professional naturalist's disinterestedness and experimental method. Thoreau sought ecstasy.

This perfect satisfaction could not always be found; there were inevitable days of bleakness, dissatisfaction, and weakness. But Thoreau, using nature and God as instruments of personal power and happiness, was able to create on paper his own life of satisfaction, to retain in words the aura of some bygone ecstasy he had found through nature. He was able, thus, to make a life by writing it. This was his great instrument, a prose that always took the form of personal experience, a prose created wholly out of remembrance and its transfiguration, a prose in which the word sought not only to commemorate a thing but to replace it. What had been lost could always be found again on the page, and what had merely been wished for could be described as if it were remembered. Memory was Thoreau's imagination to the point where it relived the original so intensely that it replaced it as style. The dreaming mind of the writer, remembering his life, created it.

But this called for the most relentless control over life by style, by an attentiveness to the uses of words that quite wore him out, by calculated epigrams, puns, paradoxes, plays on words, ingenuities, quotations, that, as he complained in his journal of 1854, were his faults of style. He had practiced these "faults of style" so long that he had become weary of his own strategy, for even the most devoted reader of Thoreau is likely to see through his literary tricks. But these "tricks," or "faults of style," are the essence of Thoreau's genius and the reason for his enduring appeal. They have an extraordinary ability to evoke the moment, the instant flash of experience, to give us the taste of existence itself. They give us the glory of a moment—single, concrete, singular.

Thoreau was always, I think, a young man, and certainly oriented, as Thornton Wilder put it, to childhood. He addressed his most famous book to "poor students," and his most admiring readers, whether they are young or not, always recognize the inner feeling of youth in his pages—the absoluteness of his impatience with authority and his all too conscious revolt against it, the natural vagabondage, the faith in some infinite world just over the next horizon. Students recognize in Henry Thoreau a classic near their own age and condition.

All his feelings are absolutes, as his political ideals will be. There is none of that subtlety, that odd and winning two-handedness, that one finds in Emerson's simultaneous obligation to both his deepest insights and to the social world he thinks in. Thoreau wrote in his journal for 1851 that "no experience which I have today comes up to, or is comparable with, the experiences of my boyhood. . . . As far back as I can remember I have unconsciously referred to the experiences of a previous state of existence. . . . Formerly, methought, nature developed as I developed, and grew up with me. My life was ecstasy. In youth, before I lost any of my senses, I can remember that I was all alive, and inhabited my body with inexpressible satisfaction."

This happiness is what Thoreau's admirers turn to him for—it is a special consonance of feeling between the pilgrim and his landscape. And it was not so much written as rewritten; whatever the moment originally was, his expression of it was forged, fabricated, worked over and over, soldered together, you might say, from fragmentary responses, to make those single sentences that were Thoreau's highest achievement, and indeed, his highest aim. For *in* such sentences, and not just *by* those sentences, a man could live. Transcendentalism rested on style. Each of Thoreau's sentences is a culmination of his life, the fruit of his hallucinated attachment to the visible world; each was a precious particle of existence, existence pure, the life of Thoreau at the very heart. Each was victory over the long, unconscious loneliness; and how many people, with far more happiness in others than Thoreau ever wanted or expected, can say that their life is all victory? how many can anticipate a succession of victories? In the end was the word, always the word:

> When I was four years old, as I well remember, I was brought from Boston to this my native town, through these very woods and fields, to the pond. It is one of the oldest scenes stamped on my memory. And tonight my flute has waked the echoes over that very water. The pines still stand here older than I; or, if some have fallen, I have cooked my supper with their stumps, and a new growth is rising all around, preparing another aspect for new infant eyes. Almost the same johnwort springs from the same perennial root in this pasture, and even I have at length helped to clothe that fabulous landscape of my infant dreams, and one of the results of my presence and influence is seen in these bean leaves, corn blades, and potato vines.

A student once wrote in a paper on Thoreau: "This man, too honest, too physically aware to fashion an imagined scene, . . . searched to exhaustion a scene that sometimes appeared empty." But another student, as if to answer this, noted that after writing *Walden* Thoreau could look about him, as we do today when we visit Walden Pond, with the feeling that this environment had been changed by his writing the book. Thoreau did create and recreate Walden Pond; the total attachment to that bit of land, from the hut which became for him, Ellery Channing said, the wooden inkstand in which he lived—this attachment is as total and single in its all-absorbing attentiveness as a baby's to its mother, as a prisoner to his cell. *Walden* is the record of a love blind to everything but what it can gather from that love, to everything but the force of its will. That is why those to whom their own will still stands supreme, to whom freedom is the freedom of *their* will, solitary but sovereign, can recognize in *Walden* the youthful climate of feeling that is touched by doom but not by tragedy—to whom death seems easier than any blow whatever from the social compact.

For youth the center of the world is itself, and the center is bright with the excitement of the will. There is no drama like that of being young, for then each experience can be overwhelming. Thoreau knew how to be young. He knew, as he said, how to live deep and suck all the marrow out of life. "I went to the woods because I wished to live deliberately, to front only the essential facts of life, and see if I could not learn what it had to teach, and not, when I came to die, to discover that I had not lived. I did not wish to live what was not life, living is so dear; nor did I wish to practise resignation, unless it was quite necessary." That is youth speaking, for only youth thinks that it can live by deliberation, that a man's whole happiness can be planned like a day off, that perfect satisfaction can be achieved without any friction whatever, without friends, without sex, with a God who is always and only the perfect friend, and all this in relation to a piece of land, a pond, practicing the gospel of perfection. Yet only youth ever feels so alone, and being alone, burns to *create* its life—where so many people merely spend theirs. Thoreau's greatness lies in his genius for evoking the moment, in sentence after sentence each of which is like a moment.

For only the individual in the most private accesses of his experience knows what a moment is; it is a unit too small for history, too precious for society. It belongs only to the private consciousness. And Thoreau's predominating aim was to save his life, not to spend it, to be as economical about his life as his maiden aunts were about the sugar in the boarding house they ran. He wanted to live, to live supremely, and always on his own terms, saving his life for still higher things as he went.

Here is where the State comes in. Nature, as we know, Thoreau could always transcendentalize. No storms or solitude or discomfort could turn him out of his fanatical control there. He felt at home in the world of savages. If he was in any sense the scientist he occasionally wanted to be, it was when he felt superior and untouched by dumb things in nature. The only object in nature that seems genuinely to have frightened him was Mount Katahdin in Maine. Describing the night he spent on the summit, he significantly confessed: "I stand in awe of my body, this matter to which I am bound has become so strange to me. I fear not spirits, ghosts, of which I am one . . . but I fear bodies, I tremble to meet them. What is this Titan that has possession of me? Talk of our life in nature —daily to be shown matter, to come in contact with it— rocks, trees, wind on our cheeks! the *solid* earth, the *actual* world! the *common sense!* Contact! *Contact!* Who are we? *where* are we?"

Still, he could always get off that mountain and return to the village of which he said, "I could write a book called Concord," and which he began to see wholly as the book he was writing in his journal. But the State, which to begin with was represented by other men he could not always ignore—this was to become the Other that he could not domesticate as he did God, Nature, and other men's books. In chapter 8 of *Walden*, "The Village," he describes his arrest (July, 1846) as he was on his way to the cobbler's. He was arrested for not paying the poll tax that in those days was still exacted by the state in behalf of the church. Thoreau's father had been enrolled in the church, and Thoreau's own name should not have been on the roll. He spent a peaceful, dreamy night in jail. In "Civil Disobedience" he reports that "the night in prison was novel and interesting enough. . . . It was like travelling into a far country, such as I had never expected to behold, to lie there for one night. . . . It was to see my native village in the light of the Middle Ages, and our Concord was turned into a Rhine stream, and visions of knights and castles passed before me." At the suggestion of the Concord selectmen, he filed a statement after he had demanded that his name be dropped from the church rolls: KNOW ALL MEN BY THESE PRESENTS THAT I, HENRY THOREAU, DO NOT WISH TO BE REGARDED AS A MEMBER OF ANY INCORPORATED SOCIETY WHICH I HAVE NOT JOINED. The experience was not a traumatic one, and on being released he "returned to the woods in season to get my dinner of huckleberries on Fair Haven Hill." But he says truly, "I was never molested by any person but those who represented the State."

In *Walden* Thoreau was to say of his prison experience that it showed the inability of society to stand "odd fellows" like himself. In the essay "Civil Disobedience," 1849, he was to say in a most superior way that the State supposed "I was mere flesh and blood and bones, to be locked up," and since it could not recognize that his immortal spirit was free, "I saw that the State was half-witted, that it was timid as a lone woman with her silver spoons . . . and I lost all my remaining respect for it, and pitied it."

But what gives "Civil Disobedience" its urgency is that between 1846, when he was arrested for a tax he should have paid in 1840, and 1848, when he wrote it, the State had ceased to be his friend the Concord sheriff, Sam Staples, who so pleasantly took him off to the local hoosegow, but the United States government, which, under the leadership of imperialists like President James Polk and the Southern planters who were determined to add new land for their cotton culture, was making war on Mexico and would take away half its territory in the form of California, Texas, Arizona, and New Mexico. The Mexican War was openly one for plunder, as Lincoln and many other Americans charged. But it was the first significant shock to Thoreau's rather complacent position that the individual can be free, as free as he likes, in and for himself, though his neighbors think him odd. Oddity, however, was no longer enough to sustain total independence from society. Despite Thoreau's opposition to slavery in principle, he knew no Negroes, had never experienced the slightest social oppression. He was a radical individualist very well able to support this position in Concord; he had a share in the family's pencil business, but was not confined by it, and he was indeed as free as air—free to walk about all day long as he pleased, free to build himself a shack on Walden Pond and there prepare to write a book, free to walk home any night for supper at the family boarding house. Up until the Mexican War—and even more urgently, the Fugitive Slave Law of 1850 and finally John Brown's raid on Harpers Ferry in 1859—Thoreau's only social antagonist was the disapproval, mockery, or indifference of his neighbors in Concord. He never knew what the struggle of modern politics can mean for people who identify and associate with each other because they recognize their common condition. Thoreau was a pure idealist, living on principle—typical of New England in his condescension to the Irish immigrants, properly indignant about slavery in far-off Mississippi, but otherwise, as he wrote *Walden* to prove, a man who proposed to teach others to be as free of society as himself.

Civil Disobedience is stirring, especially today, because of the urgency of its personal morality. As is usual with

Thoreau, he seems to be putting his whole soul into the protest against injustice committed by the state. He affirms the absolute right of the individual to obey his own conscience in defiance of an unknown law. But despite his usual personal heat, he tends to moralize the subject wholly and to make it not really serious. He makes a totally ridiculous object of the State, he turns its demands on him into a pure affront, and is telling it to stop being so pretentious and please to disappear. This is certainly refreshing. But anyone who thinks it is a guide to his own political action these days will have to defend the total literary anarchism that is behind it. And it is no use, in this particular, identifying Gandhi with it, for Gandhi, as a young leader of the oppressed Indians in South Africa, was looking for some political strategy by which to resist a totally oppressive racist regime. There were no laws to protect the Indians. Thoreau's essay is a noble, ringing reiteration of the highest religious individualism as a self-evident social principle. The absolute freedom of the individual like himself is his highest good, and the State is not so much the oppressor of this individual as his rival. How dare this Power get in my way? For Thoreau the problem is simply one of putting the highest possible value on the individual rather than on the state. This is urgent because we are all individuals first, and because it is sometimes necessary to obey oneself rather than the State. But for the greatest part, Thoreau is not aware that the individual's problem may be how to resist his state when he is already so much bound up with it. He can hardly just turn his back on it.

The significantly political passages in the essay have to do with what Thoreau calls slavery in Massachusetts. He of all people could not grant that property is the greatest passion and the root of most social conflicts and wars. But he insisted "that if one thousand, if one hundred, if ten men whom I could name—if ten *honest* men only—ay, if *one* Honest man, in this State of Massachusetts, *ceasing to hold slaves,* were actually to withdraw from this co-partnership, and be locked up in the county jail therefor, it would be the abolition of slavery in America." With his marvellous instinct for justice, for pure Christianity, for the deep-rooted rights of the individual soul, he said "Under a government which imprisons any unjustly, the true place for a just man is also a prison." But morally invigorating as this is, it would perhaps not have helped the fugitive slave, and the Mexican prisoner on parole, and the Indian come to plead the wrongs of his race when, as Thoreau said, they came to the prison and found the best spirits of Massachusetts there. Thoreau estimated the power of individual example beyond any other device in politics, but he did not explain how the usefulness of example could communicate itself to people who were in fact slaves, and not free.

By 1850 the fury of the coming war could already be felt in Massachusetts. The Fugitive Slave Law was made part of the compromise of 1850, and now Thoreau really exploded. "There is not one slave in Nebraska; there are perhaps a million slaves in Massachusetts." With all his uncompromising idealism he attacked every possible expediency connected with politics, and wrote: "They who have been bred in the school of politics fail now and always to face the facts. They put off the day of settlement indefinitely, and meanwhile, the debt accumulates." The "idea of turning a man into a sausage" is not worse than to obey the Fugitive Slave Law. Rhythmically, he pounded away at the State, the Press, the Church, all institutions leagued, as he felt, by this infamous conspiracy to send runaway slaves back to their masters. He mimicked the attitude of the timorous, law-obeying citizen: "Do what you will, O Government! with my wife and children . . . I will obey your commands to the letter. . . . I will peaceably pursue my chosen calling on this fair earth, until perchance, one day, when I have put on mourning for them dead, I shall have persuaded you to relent." Each sentence is, as usual, an absolute in itself; each is a distillation of Thoreau's deepest feelings. Yet it is impossible to imagine the most passionately anti-Vietnam writer saying today that, in the face of such evil, "I need not say what match I would touch, what system endeavor to blow up. . . ." We have all lived too much under the shadow of the Bomb to be persuaded by the violence of language.

Thoreau's greatest affirmation in politics (something different from a great political utterance) is, I think, *A Plea For Captain John Brown,* delivered in the Concord Town Hall on the evening of October 30, 1859. Emerson's son Edward, who heard Thoreau deliver this, said that he read his speech as if it burned him. There is nothing quite so strong elsewhere in Thoreau's work; all the dammed-up violence of the man's solitary life has come out in sympathy with Brown's violence. It is clear that Brown's attack on Harpers Ferry roused in Thoreau a powerful sense of identification. Apocalypse had come. John Brown's favorite maxim was: "without the shedding of blood there is no remission of sins." Brown's raid was exactly the kind of mad, wild, desperate, and headlong attack on the authority of the United States, on the support it gave to the slave system, that Thoreau's ecstatic individualism sympathized with. It was too violent an act for Thoreau to commit himself; he had long since given up the use of firearms, and was more or less of a vegetarian. But Brown represented in the most convulsively personal way the hatred of injustice that was Thoreau's most significant political passion—and this was literally a *hatred,* more so than he could acknowledge to himself, a hatred of anyone as well as anything that marred the perfect design of his all-too-severe moral principles.

All his life, Thoreau had been saying that there are two realms. One is of grace, which is a gift and so belongs only to the gifted; the other is of mediocrity. One is of freedom, which is the absolute value because only the gifted can follow it into the infinite where its beauty is made fully manifest; the other of acquiescence and conformism, another word for which is stupidity. One is of God, whom His elect, the most gifted, know as no one else can ever know Him; the other is of the tyranny exacted by the mediocre in society. John Brown, whom all the leading historians, judges, lawyers, and respectable people solidly denounced as mad; John Brown, who indeed had so much madness in his background, nevertheless represented to Thoreau the gifted man's, the ideal Puritan's, outraged inability to compromise between these two realms. Nothing is worse than evil except the toleration of it, thought John Brown, and so he tried to strike at evil itself. This directness proved his moral genius to Thoreau. Then, as the State of Virginia and the Government of the United States rallied all its forces to crush this man and to hang him, it turned out, to Thoreau's horror, that this exceptional man was not understood. The State, which would do nothing to respect the slave's human rights, and had in deference to Southern opinion acknowledged its duty to send back every runaway slave, would indeed obliterate John Brown with an energy that it had never showed in defense of helpless human beings.

It was this that roused Thoreau to the burning exaltation that fills *A Plea For Captain John Brown*. He had found his hero in the man of action who proclaimed that his action was only the force of the highest principles. Thoreau's "plea" indeed pleads principle as the irresistible force. The pure, vehement personalism that had been Thoreau's life, in words, now sees itself turning into deeds. The pure love of Christ, striking against obstinately uncomprehending, resisting human heads, turns into pure wrath. God has only certain appointed souls to speak and fight for Him, and that is the secret of New England. "We aspire to be something more than stupid and timid chattels, pretending to read history and our Bibles, but desecrating every house and every day we breathe in. . . . At least a million of the free inhabitants of the United States would have rejoiced if he had succeeded. . . . Though we wear no crape, the thought of that man's position and probable fate is spoiling many a man's day here at the North for other thinking. If anyone who has seen him here can pursue successfully any other train of thought, I do not know what he is made of. If there is any such who gets his usual allowance of sleep, I will warrant him to fatten easily under any circumstances which do not touch his body or his purse." But for himself, Thoreau added, "I put a piece of paper and a pencil under my pillow, and when I could not sleep I wrote in the dark."

He wrote in the dark. Writing was what he had lived for, lived by, lived in. And now, when his great friend was being hanged in Charlestown prison, he could only speak for. The word was light, the word was the Church, and now the word was the deed. This was Thoreau's only contribution to the struggle that was not for John Brown's body but for righteousness. He called the compromisers "mere figureheads upon a hulk, with livers in the place of hearts." He said of the organized Church that it always "excommunicates Christ while it exists." He called the government this most *hypocritical* and *diabolical* government, and mimicked its saying to protesters like himself: "What do you assault me for? Am I not an honest man? Cease agitation on this subject, or I will make a slave of you, too, or else hang you." He said, "I am here to plead this cause with you. I plead not for his life, but for his character—his immortal life; and so it becomes your cause wholly, and is not his in the least. Some eighteen hundred years ago Christ was crucified; this morning, perchance, Captain Brown was hung. These are the two ends of a chain which is not without its links."

There was nothing Thoreau could do except to *say* these things. Brown, who was quite a sayer himself, had said to the court: "Had I so interfered in behalf of the rich, the powerful, the intelligent, the so-called great . . . it would have been all right . . . I am yet too young to understand that God is any respecter of persons. I believe that to have interfered as I have done—as I have always freely admitted I have done—in defense of His despised poor, was not wrong but right."

Yet we in our day cannot forget that Brown was punished for a direct assault on the Government, for seeking to stir up an actual insurrection. By contrast, *our* martyrs, in the age of the Big State, the Totalitarian State, the All-Demanding State, have been innocent children like Anne Frank, who died in concentration camps simply because they were Jews; isolated German soldiers like Franz Jägerstätter, beheaded because they would not kill; theologians like Dietrich Bonhoeffer, executed because they openly opposed killing; the Polish priest Maximilian Kolbe, who took another man's place in one of the "starvation cells" at Auschwitz and died after weeks of agony. If we have any moral heroes and imminent martyrs today, it is not men of violence, no matter how holy the cause seems to them, but Russian writers and poets who are locked up for years in Arctic camps for sending their manuscripts out of the country; American scientists who refuse to aid in the destruction of Vietnam and its people; young students who believe in peace, live by peace, and act for peace. Thoreau said that "the cost of a thing is the amount of what I will call life which is required to be exchanged for it," and the cost of nonviolence itself is sometimes so great in the face of the powerful twentieth-century state that Thoreau, who identified power only with individual spiritual power, does not help us in the face of the state power which we both need for our welfare and dread for its power over lives.

Thoreau did not anticipate the modern state. He distrusted it even more absolutely than did Jesus in the days when Rome was the greatest power on earth. Jesus counseled—Render unto Caesar the things that are Caesar's. Not only would Thoreau not compromise with the State; he would not recognize it. Near his end, when the Civil War broke out, he advised an abolitionist friend to "ignore Fort Sumter, and old Abe, and all that; for that is just the most fatal, and indeed, the only fatal weapon you can direct against evil, ever. . . ." In short—"Be ye perfect, even as your Father in Heaven is perfect." That was all the power Thoreau knew and believed in, outside of the writer's power that he lived by. He would not have believed it possible that the United States would be reading and applauding Thoreau without any sense of irony. The greatest irony is that this American government has become just as self-righteous as Thoreau thought the individual should be.

Thoreau, Charles Ives, and Contemporary Music

Philip Corner

THERE IS
AN INCREDIBLE FLUX OF
NOVELTY INTO THE WORLD,
AND YET WE TOLERATE
   INCREDIBLE DULLNESS.

THE STUDY OF NATURE
MAY TEND TO
MAKE ONE DOGMATIC
BUT THE LOVE
OF NATURE SURELY
         DOES NOT.

Charles Ives would certainly have opposed the war in Vietnam.

A day in 1846 Henry Thoreau found himself imprisoned, in Concord, Mass., for refusing to pay tax.

He felt keenly the encroachment of a government which acted little on the basis of equitability or justice. And he himself had come close to believing against any form of government whatsoever.

If the view of the composer Ives was not quite so extreme, he was equally committed to ideals—the same ideals. His sense of the democratic was in the tradition of the New England Town Meeting.

These larger human involvements by philosopher-artists have much meaning for us. —As much as the pages they left. —Indeed, the quality of their lives is a prime necessity in the creation of these pages.

We can be most specific: being more than simply inspiring personal examples; the *content* of their concern, remains relevant.

> THERE COMES FROM CONCORD
> AN OFFER TO EVERY MAN—
> THE CHOICE BETWEEN
> REPOSE AND TRUTH.

Thoreau's "Civil Disobedience" was explicit in condemning both slavery and the American aggression against Mexico.

—A great parallel! Those two burning issues of *this* day (their direct descendents).

Will we be as much? Will we each of us match that record of how a man acts in such times?

> IT MATTERS NOT ONE JOT,
> PROVIDED THE CAUSE
> OF PERSONAL LOYALTY TO A
> CAUSE BE STEADFASTLY
> PURSUED, WHAT THE SPECIAL
> CHARACTERISTICS OF THE
> STYLE OF THE MUSIC MAY BE.

WHAT IS THE PRICE CURRENT
OF AN HONEST MAN AND A
PATRIOT TODAY?

(Thoreau)   (Ives)
IN OTHER WORDS, WHEN A   THE CLEAR PICTURE OF
SIXTH OF THE POPULATION   INHUMANITY FORCED ON THE
OF A NATION WHICH HAS   WORLD . . . THE FIRST
UNDERTAKEN TO BE THE   NEWS OF THE KAISER'S

REFUGE OF LIBERTY ARE
SLAVES, AND A WHOLE
COUNTRY IS UNJUSTLY
OVERRUN AND CONQUERED BY
A FOREIGN ARMY . . .
I THINK THAT IT IS NOT
TOO SOON TO REBEL AND
REVOLUTIONIZE.

HOG-MARCH THROUGH
BELGIUM.

WHAT MAKES THIS DUTY THE
MORE URGENT IS THE FACT
THAT THE COUNTRY SO
OVERRUN IS NOT OUR OWN,
BUT OURS IS THE
INVADING ARMY.

SO NOW THE ONE BIG THING
FOR THE PEOPLE IN THE
WORLD TODAY IS TO MAKE
IT A MAN'S WORLD AND NOT A
SNEAKTHIEVING, SISSY,
MOLLYCODDLE, SUSPICIOUS
WORLD TO LIVE AND DIE IN.

As on my first page they speak of each other, here they both
speak together, and for now.

I THINK THAT WE SHOULD BE
MEN FIRST, AND SUBJECTS
AFTERWARD.

Philosophic: breakdown the thought—reality dualism.
    It is not enough if you do not *act* it. (It may not be
    anything at all.) "No ideas except in things," said the
    poet William Carlos Williams.
Personal: the necessary consequences of an uncompromis-
    ing life.
The recluse who inspired
revolutionaries.

The intellectual who was
a woodsman.

I would not be exaggerating to say that the jail-house was the negative pole of which Walden Pond was the positive, the axis being Thoreau's own integrity and his knowledge of the accord between self and nature, and how contemplation is led out into the world.

HIS TEMPERAMENT COM-
MITTED HIM TO ACTION, HIS
FAITH TO CONTEMPLATION.

Read the "Essays Before a Sonata," wherein Ives shares his sense of vigorous immediacy which yet can contain Man's entire past: the transcendent thought from sages of China and Ancient Greece, and with them a whole line of New England preachers. Wisdom of the spirit which embraces with no lessening of that multifarious everyday world containing baseball, business, picnics, and marching bands.

(About Ives) : firmly and enthusiastically rooted in the life of his time—yet with an encompassing perspective— *and* the most surely affirmed integrity of his person.

(About Thoreau) : personification of individualism to the point of iconoclasm, he was nevertheless intensely engaged in the affairs of the world. (About both of them) : That Thoreau, a man of solitude and a liver in nature, equally an observer of natural phenomena and a reader of classics, a man reported to be not excessively sociable, should make himself a model of social consciousness shows the dimensions which are able to be brought into essential oneness.

—morning meditation at Walden Pond and Civil Disobedience in town—not only reconcilable, but together in a flow of mutual effects and consequences.

THE ONLY OBLIGATION
WHICH I HAVE A RIGHT TO
ASSUME IS TO DO AT ANY
TIME WHAT I THINK RIGHT.

This striking blend of opposite concerns: this degree of complexity harmonized to the point of paradox: with Ives it is the same. In expression; in his music.

these poles:

the active, complex and dynamic. Whitmanesque . . .
the simple and tranquil, quiescent—as if oriental . . .

WALT WHITMAN
who was also both!

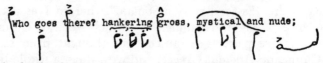

At *both* of these extreme points, his is more developed than any other music of this century. (Whole-tone scale; ostinati and permutated repetition; polyrhythms, multitonality, freed of keys, themes, great dissonance.)

Perhaps there *is* no paradox, and the extremes are the same.

HE KNOWS, and all is reconciled.

He calls them THE ANTIPODES in his great song. . . . whole gamut in details; all harmonized . . .

> "Do I contradict myself?
> Very well then, I contradict myself,
> (I am large, I contain multitudes)."

As Thoreau did it as he lived it.

Ives wrote Transcendent—perhaps this is what it was that they call a philosophical movement!

And Ives lived it too. With the one half of his life in the insurance business. ! so improbable an endeavor . . . that *that* was where he could put himself, put his heart. Yet he was in it fully; he believed in it; he found there a field for vigor and for creative contributions. Even for ideals. (Allow me to defer comment on this.)

For now, *for the contact of the creative spirit with the substance of the real world,* I will call the firm of Ives & Myrick: "CHARLES IVES'S WALDEN POND."

> PERHAPS THE BIRTH OF ART WILL TAKE PLACE AT THE MOMENT IN WHICH THE LAST MAN WHO IS WILLING TO MAKE A LIVING OUT OF ART IS GONE FOREVER.

This man of unlimited interests.
:Theoretical papers on acoustics and harmony.
:Political and social essays.
—he circulated a proposal for a 20th Amendment to the Constitution—conceived of the League of Nations beginning Man's Progress to a People's World Nation (all of these things getting into expression within the music).
And so transcends another duality: Music in its quality of timelessness—and its essential rootedness in immediacy.

Whitman: "I resist anything better than my own diversity."

> DISTINGUISHING BETWEEN
> THE COMPLEXITY OF NATURE,
> WHICH TEACHES FREEDOM,
> AND THE COMPLEXITY OF
> MATERIALISM, WHICH
> TEACHES SLAVERY.

Ives's unparalleled scope: of expression, of technique, of exploration—it is the consequence of his immersion in detail—full living reality, turning the concrete into mind-stuff, building complexities the way nature grows them: Elaboration Above Simplicity.

This is quite a message for an age which persists in starting *from* abstractions.

In the 19th Century it seemed that Boston was cosmopolitan and Concord provincial; now it seems otherwise. The universal is discovered everywhere in some particular.
IT IS NOT WORTHWHILE TO
GO ROUND THE WORLD TO
COUNT THE CATS IN
ZANZIBAR.
. . . and if Ives is in any sense a "Nationalist" he is the one—with the possible only exception of Bartok, who has in this century successfully confronted this issue.

FOR IF HE HAS LIVED SINCERELY, IT MUST HAVE BEEN IN A DISTANT LAND TO ME.

WITH THIS ASSURANCE HIS MUSIC WILL HAVE EVERYTHING IT SHOULD OF SINCERITY, NOBILITY, STRENGTH, AND BEAUTY, NO MATTER HOW IT SOUNDS; AND IF WITH THIS HE IS TRUE TO NONE BUT THE HIGHEST OF AMERICAN IDEALS (THAT IS, THE IDEALS ONLY THAT COINCIDE WITH HIS SPIRITUAL CONSCIOUSNESS) HIS MUSIC WILL BE TRUE TO ITSELF AND INCIDENTALLY AMERICAN.

This has something to do with Ives's distinction between the substantial core and the surface mannerism.

SUBSTANCE TENDS TO CREATE AFFECTION, MANNER PREJUDICE.

DO WE CALL THIS THE LAND OF THE FREE? WHAT IS IT TO BE FREE FROM KING GEORGE AND CONTINUE THE SLAVES OF KING PREJUDICE?

A TRUE LOVE OF COUNTRY IS LIKELY TO BE SO BIG THAT IT WILL EMBRACE THE VIRTUE ONE SEES IN OTHER COUNTRIES.

SUBSTANCE CAN BE EXPRESSED IN MUSIC . . . IT IS THE ONLY VALUABLE THING IN IT. SUBSTANCE HAS SOMETHING TO DO WITH CHARACTER. THE SUBSTANCE OF A TUNE COMES FROM SOMEWHERE NEAR THE SOUL, AND THE MANNER COMES FROM GOD KNOWS WHERE.

(first thoughts on this subject): Thoreau and Ives: of concern to demonstrate the relation . . . to "put" them together. The label-word—"Transcendentalism." But I stopped myself before I could reach that scholarly textbook. Are the sounds of Ives. . . . Are the words of Thoreau . . . not transcendental enough? If I would be before them and not be able to know that, what could any professor tell me? In Ives's essay—he has enough insights without making a system. As he tells his professor-critics: "Your Thoreau is not my Thoreau."

THERE IS ONLY ONE WAY,
WE SAY; BUT THERE ARE AS
MANY WAYS AS CAN BE
DRAWN RADII FROM ONE
CENTER.
IF MEN COULD COMBINE THUS
EARNESTLY AND PATIENTLY
AND HARMONIOUSLY TO
SOME REALLY WORTHY END,
WHAT MIGHT THEY NOT
ACCOMPLISH?

I could feel the great synthesis, the sense of the musical sounds I have loved for years, as if Thoreau was telling me in his words about them—he, who could not have heard them, teaching me.

The touch of the world flowing in all the shapes of the spirit. I saw in this a Yankee form of the ecstatic and virile revelations recognized in the transcendentals, from the Zen masters to the Hasidim.

So if the Word is ever the same, and the Great Too, or the Oversoul, or the 2 gods which express the nameless, are forever in the eyes and ears— (when the mote is removed) then . . . I may develop the idea that they, these two, may be together and may be the more together—in that there be nothing to *put* them together.

Let these things affect the very life itself—know Walden better than those who can quote it better.

"ON THE NECESSITY OF CIVIL DISOBEDIENCE"—words to shake up your soul. You must understand this more than scholarship, by your own day in jail.

IT MAY BE POSSIBLE THAT A DAY IN A KANSAS WHEAT FIELD WILL DO MORE FOR [THE AMERICAN COMPOSER] THAN 3 YEARS IN ROME.

I HAVE EXPERIENCED A GREAT FULLNESS OF LIFE IN BUSINESS.

Let me then know nothing of the philosophical schools —in the spirit of Thoreau being no scholastic naturalist— but writing his great nature book.

UNDER A GOVERNMENT WHICH IMPRISONS ANY UNJUSTLY, THE TRUE PLACE FOR A JUST MAN IS ALSO A PRISON.

THE FABRIC OF EXISTENCE WEAVES ITSELF WHOLE.

Now I could say: Surely they are closely related! *They are both Americans.* Does that sound trivial? . . . or even offensive? . . . what I mean: So much their own selves. They are both so supremely and uniquely "individuals"; so not-*only* "Americans."

Our Nationalism is not the uniformity of elsewhere— except on 4th of July the Stars & Stripes America and HUAC! And Never with great art.

If it appears that there has ever been here the kind of cultural coherence as, say, in Europe, this is an illusion. There is, yes, an ersatz importation, the institutionalized "genteel tradition" that every great American creator, and certainly our two, had to fight against, had to get through, had to dig through the thick dead foreign layer to the source, buried somewhere in the ground where the Indians were exterminated.

If we do not identify through the continuity of a consistent tradition, this is no loss. It is freedom, as we can as individuals work from *any* starting-point toward the One-Center. It is this, I believe, which has permitted the music of Ives (not, as has been stated, to be full of flaws and "lapses from good taste") but—to stand as an achievement of unparalleled scope.

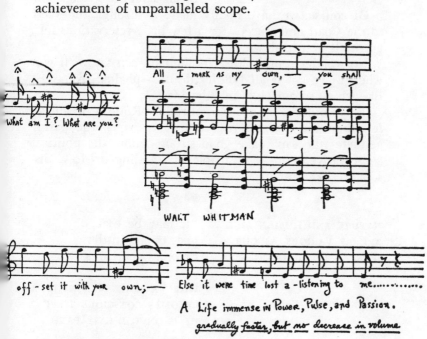

MY PURPOSE IN GOING TO
WALDEN POND WAS NOT TO
LIVE CHEAPLY NOR TO LIVE
DEARLY THERE, BUT TO
TRANSACT SOME PRIVATE
BUSINESS WITH THE FEWEST
POSSIBLE OBSTACLES.

There is a "Tradition of the New"; in art-critic Harold Rosenberg's book he uses the image of the "redcoats" making war on revolutionary America, or trying to, playing the war game as on the mapped-out battlefields of Europe. Using the 12 tone system— (any numbers will do, *system*atically). On any number of campuses they are still trying to chart the wilderness.

AN ITCH TO BE ORIGINAL
WITH NOTHING BUT NUMBERS
TO BE ORIGINAL WITH.

Of course, we have finally made it through the West to the Coast and, except for a few little reservations left, got it all pinned down.

No wonder some soldier in Vietnam can say we'll win when we've got it all bulldozed and asphalted over—just like we do to ourselves in suburbia.

This would be the place to introduce Rollo, a personage found in the margins of Ives's manuscripts, the parlor aesthete who can't take good strong sound, the political conservative, who is incapable of standing up to a dissonance like a man.

NATURE AND HUMAN LIFE
ARE AS VARIOUS AS OUR
SEVERAL CONSTITUTIONS.

"It may be that when a poet or a whistler becomes conscious"

WHEN A POET OR WHISTLER
BECOMES CONSCIOUS THAT
HE IS ON THE EASY PATH

"that he is in the easy path of any particular idiom— that he is helplessly prejudiced in favor of any particular means of expression—"

THAT HE FAVORS A CONTRA-
PUNTAL GROOVE, A SOUND-
COLORING ONE,

"that his manner can be
catalogued as modern or
classic—that he favors
a contrapuntal groove,
a sound-coloring one,"

A SUCCESSFUL ONE

"a sensuous one, a successful one, or a melodious one
(whatever that means) —
that his interests lie in the
French school or the Ger-
man school, or the school of
Saturn—that he is involved
in this particular 'that' or
that particular 'this,' or in
any particular brand of
emotional complexes—in a
word, when he becomes
conscious that his style is
'his personal own,' that it
has monopolized a geo-
graphical part of the world's
sensibilities—then it may
be that the value of his
substance is not growing,
that it even may have
started on its way back-
wards; it may be that he is
trading an inspiration of a
bad habit, and, finally,
that he is reaching fame,

permanence, or some other undervalue, and that he is getting farther and farther from a perfect truth."

TRADING INSPIRATION FOR A BAD HABIT.

Henry Cowell says, in his biography of Ives: "To experience and explore has never been revolutionary for an American; he is at home in the unregulated and untried."

IF YOU HAVE ANY ENTERPRISE BEFORE YOU, TRY IT IN YOUR OLD CLOTHES.

EVERYONE SHOULD HAVE THE OPPORTUNITY OF NOT BEING OVER-INFLUENCED.

NO YARD! BUT UNFENCED NATURE REACHING UP TO YOUR VERY SILLS.

One could hardly talk about Ives and about Thoreau while wearing the acceptable starched and tied formal dress.

A MAN WHO HAS AT LENGTH FOUND SOMETHING TO DO, WILL NOT NEED TO GET A SUIT TO DO IT IN.

YOU CANNOT SET AN ART OFF IN THE CORNER, AND HOPE FOR IT TO HAVE VITALITY, REALITY, AND SUBSTANCE.

THERE CAN BE NOTHING EXCLUSIVE ABOUT A SUBSTANTIAL ART.

So I will need not make any relationships which do not occur of themselves. Not even trying—how many ideas and things are drawn together.

IT COMES DIRECTLY OUT OF THE HEART OF EXPERIENCE OF LIFE AND THINKING ABOUT LIFE AND LIVING LIFE.

UNJUST LAWS EXIST. SHALL
WE BE CONTENT TO OBEY
THEM?

THE "UNITY OF DRESS" FOR
A MAN AT A BALL REQUIRES
A COLLAR, YET HE COULD
DANCE BETTER WITHOUT IT.

A WISE MAN WILL ONLY BE
USEFUL AS A MAN.

People are fond of admitting all of Ives's innovations:
"Yes . . . but . . ." Thirty years late our critics and pro-
fessionals are still condescending, though they've caught
up enough to "appreciate" him.

When I was involved in presenting concerts of this music
I heard, "Everyone's interested in Ives, but not to go and
hear him." (Though that situation is gradually changing—
at least for him.) After all this time, listeners should be
beyond both the initial shocked incomprehension, and the
phase of respectful enumeration of the innovations. Nothing less than to be able to *hear* the music, to experience
how marvelous it is.

Yet he says in "Grantchester" when he evokes the Faun
that "the Classics are not dead." What did Thoreau read
in his words? Classics for them meant more than the provincial nonsense of "the Western Heritage." Rather they in-
clude the Vedas, and the Chinese philosopher-kings. They
would have evidently accepted anything and everything of
value that they could have known about—as there is no
excuse for our not doing.

Is ♪♪♪ ♩ banged out on Bronson Alcott's beat-up
piano in Concord less the real Beethoven
than—than what?—Than Leonard Bernstein talking about
the symphony on TV? Or would one have the sterile abstractions of the theory classrooms?

And does Ives not really, after all, accept the tradition?
But the *real* tradition—accepted—truly—for what lives in
the present.

And then he puts Beethoven's Fifth into everything he writes. He knows all the good things humanity has left behind—laid up for his, and our, uses. *Not* to be sacrificed to, lest the world be corrupted by a single true idea.

The academic stupidly uses the masterpieces to limit possibilities, as models of manner rather than in- imitable portions of sub- stance, and thus is shown how that kind of teacher, like the critics, has himself no understanding of these worthy things.

The past will only be equalled (and will again and again be equalled) in ever new shapes.

I believe that it is Ives's kind of building upon the riches of the past which is the true respect for it; and not the conservative who is "upholding civilization" and per- haps killing, or condoning, to hold up this Christian Culture.

"It is not only in the arts that the Past is subject to misuse." (Thoreau)

THE GOVERNMENT ITSELF,
WHICH IS ONLY THE MODE
WHICH THE PEOPLE HAVE
CHOSEN TO EXECUTE
THEIR WILL, IS
EQUALLY LIABLE TO BE
ABUSED AND PERVERTED BE-
FORE THE PEOPLE CAN ACT
THROUGH IT.

(Ives)

PROPERTY, IN THE NAME OF
EFFICIENCY, IS TRYING TO
GET CONTROL OF THE WAR
MACHINERY, AND SO MORE
EFFECTIVELY ESTABLISH
ITSELF IN CONTROL OF THIS
COUNTRY.

(1914)
"Who gets it in the neck?
The Politicians?

NO, THE PEOPLE.
Who has the whole say in
all the countries? The
People?

NO, THE POLITICIANS."

UNDER THE NAME OF ORDER
AND CIVIL GOVERNMENT, WE
ARE ALL MADE AT LAST TO
PAY HOMAGE TO AND SUP-
PORT OUR MEANNESS.
WITNESS THE PRESENT   witness the *present* war
MEXICAN WAR, THE WORK
OF COMPARATIVELY FEW
INDIVIDUALS USING THE
STANDING GOVERNMENT AS
THEIR TOOL, FOR, IN THE
OUTSET THE PEOPLE WOULD
NOT HAVE CONSENTED TO
THIS MEASURE.

Said Mr. Lincoln, "U.S. involvement in Mexico at this
time is wholly unwarranted intrusion undertaken by us for
plainly imperialist purposes. We have absolutely no right
to be in Mexico and my sympathies are entirely with the
Mexican people. The right of the people of any country
to settle their own affairs is a most valuable—a most sacred
right."

THOUGH THE YOUTH AT LAST
GROWS INDIFFERENT, THE
LAWS OF THE UNIVERSE ARE
NOT INDIFFERENT, AND ARE
FOREVER ON THE SIDE OF
THE MOST SENSITIVE.

IN THE HISTORY OF THIS
YOUTHFUL WORLD, THE BEST
PRODUCT THAT HUMAN BE-
INGS CAN BOAST OF IS
PROBABLY BEETHOVEN.

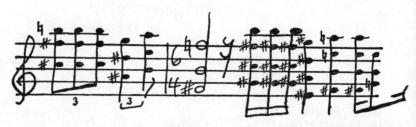

BUT MAYBE EVEN HIS ART IS
AS NOTHING IN COMPARISON
WITH THE FUTURE PRODUCT
OF SOME COAL-MINER'S SOUL
IN THE 41ST CENTURY.

Who makes war? The People?
NO, THE POLITICIANS.

THIS AMERICAN GOVERNMENT
—WHAT IS IT BUT A TRADI-
TION, THOUGH A RECENT ONE,
ENDEAVORING TO TRANSMIT
ITSELF UNIMPAIRED TO
POSTERITY, BUT EACH
INSTANT LOSING SOME OF
ITS INTEGRITY?

"Let us not, in music at least, make the same error."

HOW DOES IT BECOME A MAN
TO BEHAVE TOWARD THIS
AMERICAN GOVERNMENT
TODAY?
I ANSWER, THAT HE CANNOT
WITHOUT DISGRACE BE
ASSOCIATED WITH IT.

Thoreau said that the past enterprises are always abandoned by the next generation. No doubt he included himself! If we respect ourselves, then we may find out what is respectable in the past, and most significantly, we will then respect the future.

Coming to America, Arnold Schönberg said that he had found the great man who "has solved the problem of how to preserve one's self. His name is Ives."

YET SOME CAN BE PATRIOTIC WHO HAVE NO SELF-RESPECT, AND SACRIFICE THE GREATER TO THE LESSER.

We too should be bigger than our "oeuvre," not make careers and play the ego game, give up cramming it down others' throats, especially the young—whose teachers often inflict certain sets of standards, selfishly, because of their own attachment to such. With Ives, we can trust ourselves and creations voluntarily to be let out in the world.

A SONG HAS SOME RIGHTS OF ITS OWN.

Everything one does can be only better for this, even if my music too must lie 20 years in a Danbury Barn.

A VERY FEW, AS HEROES, PATRIOTS, MARTYRS, REFORMERS IN THE GREAT SENSE, AND MEN, AND MEN, SERVE THE STATE WITH THEIR CONSCIENCES ALSO, AND SO NECESSARILY RESIST IT, FOR THE MOST PART, AND THEY ARE COMMONLY TREATED AS ENEMIES BY IT.

SOME HAVE WRITTEN A BOOK FOR MONEY: I HAVE NOT. SOME FOR FAME: I HAVE NOT. SOME FOR KINDLINGS: I HAVE NOT. IN FACT, I HAVE NOT WRITTEN A BOOK AT ALL. I HAVE MERELY CLEANED HOUSE.

Now, is it not Ives we dig for, and not his teacher, Horatio Parker, the success?

THE TRUE HUSBANDMAN WILL CEASE FROM ANXIETY

PRIZES ARE THE BADGES OF MEDIOCRITY!

. . . SACRIFICING IN HIS MIND
NOT ONLY HIS FIRST BUT
HIS LAST FRUITS ALSO.

By the way, a thing to be looked into: How could it come that this man who went into the insurance business for idealistic motives rather than to make a lot of money, who limited his income to $10,000 yearly and believed no man should take more, who donated money to New Music publishing but refused to copyright his own work, who had some of his own music printed at his expense and sent it around free, how has it come about that this music is now possessed by a commercial publisher and that it is still not, many works, generally available?

EVERYBODY WHO WANTS A
COPY IS TO HAVE ONE.
THIS MUSIC IS NOT TO MAKE
MONEY BUT TO BE KNOWN
AND HEARD. WHY SHOULD I
INTERFERE BY HANGING ON
TO SOME SORT OF PERSONAL
LEGAL RIGHT IN IT?

THERE IS AN INNATE
QUALITY IN HUMAN NATURE
WHICH GIVES MAN THE
POWER TO SENSE THE DEEPER
CAUSES, . . . ESPECIALLY IS
THIS SO IN THE SOCIAL,
ECONOMIC, AND OTHER
ESSENTIAL RELATIONS
BETWEEN MEN.

Ives's faith:—for this he gives freedom to his performers. From this courageous beginning the music world has come so far. Even when Ives's writing is extremely, and exactly, complicated—and exacting, he is far from the practice, in some contemporary circles, of the composer's proving himself by testing the players. He may rather have been thinking of the French horn player who could never keep up with the band—or who *would* never keep up. He was after the complexity and diversity; he wrote it down as he knew how. Indeterminate composition has now developed this premise to a more direct realization. This depends equally on the availability of imaginative and responsible performers—we seem to have taken a few steps in this direction.

In the 1st Piano Sonata it is written that it is "an impromptu affair"—there follow 4 variants of one measure, to give the idea. This is not to be an excuse for making things easier—not so that the N.Y. Philharmonic could play, in 1965, an avant-garde program of Feldman, Brown, and Cage, trying to fool around, make asses of themselves.

Ives would want the performers to take it to a higher level, the unfinished growing he always talks about—stand on the guru's shoulders. He once walked out on a singer who was to perform some of his songs since, he said, the man was only doing the easy ones.

ALL CHANGE IS A MIRACLE TO CONTEMPLATE, BUT IT IS A MIRACLE WHICH IS TAKING PLACE EVERY INSTANT.

———

LAW NEVER MADE MEN A WHIT MORE JUST; AND BY MEANS OF THEIR RESPECT FOR IT, EVEN THE WELL-DISPOSED ARE DAILY MADE THE AGENTS OF INJUSTICE.

A LIFE INSURANCE POLICY IS ONE OF THE DEFINITE WAYS OF SOCIETY FOR TOUGHENING ITS MORAL MUSCLES, FOR EQUALIZING ITS MISFOR-TUNES, AND HENCE—THE OLD PROBLEM—OF SUPPLYING A FUNDAMENTAL HUMAN WANT.

———

THE INSTINCTIVE REASONING OF THE MASSES HAS BEEN THE IMPELLING INFLUENCE IN SOCIAL PROGRESS.

and this is from "The

Amount to Carry," a man-
ual for insurance men.

Refer to the last page, Movement II, 1st Piano Sonata

WHO THAT HAS HEARD A	A CLEARER SCORING MIGHT
STRAIN OF MUSIC FEARED	HAVE LOWERED THE
THEN LEST HE SHOULD	THOUGHT.
SPEAK EXTRAVAGANTLY	
ANY MORE FOREVER?	

While the volumes Ives published himself (the Concord
Sonata; the 114 Songs) are painstakingly edited, are in
fact so much revised over the years as the composer added
new notes that there sometimes exist several different and
definitive versions. There are also those which were only
fragmentary and sometimes barely decipherable sketches,
requiring, in cases like the 4th Symphony, years to realize.
This is understandable, given the neglect which gave few
opportunities for any performance. To be sure, this makes
for a greater effort to get at his intention—but Ives would
not have objected! A greater range of possibilities opens
up. For instance, the works for chamber orchestra are
dense, challenging, and a bit frightening. With hard work,
as my own experience with Tone Roads Nos. 1 & 3 showed,
they need not sound like the undifferentiated mush on the
commercial recording of them.

I DO NOT SUPPOSE THAT I
HAVE ATTAINED TO   (Ives)   (The Amount to
OBSCURITY.   Carry)
                          FOR WHAT ARE TECHNICAL
                          COMPLEXITIES ANYWAY?

Slide —— back! Now you're safe

THAT'S THE EA -sy WAY!

—WHENCE DO THEY COME IF
NOT FROM THE NATURAL
EVOLUTION OF THE BUSINESS?

(Thoreau)
NEW, UNIVERSAL, AND MORE
LIBERAL LAWS WILL BEGIN
TO ESTABLISH THEMSELVES
AROUND AND WITHIN HIM;
OR THE OLD LAWS EXPANDED,
AND INTERPRETED IN HIS
FAVOR IN A MORE LIBERAL
SENSE.

(Ives)
THE WAY WILL BE SIMPLE
ENOUGH TO BE UNDERSTOOD
BY THE MANY, AND COMPLEX
ENOUGH TO BE OF SOME
VALUE TO ALL!

The line of hard work (not excluding joy—Effortful
Ecstasy!) is incompatible with the slick assurances and
pretensions of study with Nadia Boulanger. Neither with
music department chairmen who think that traditional
music education on the campus is a necessity for us; who
list the effete American name-composers whose works are
an affront to the music under discussion today and to all

the good healthy vital art of this country; who deny to Ives a worth equal to the famous names of Europe, while dismissing utterly the folk and popular music which is of such inestimable value here. It is quite evident which choices Ives would have made. And what judgments on "Thoreau Festivals" which feature the easy quotations, carefully excluding those requiring sacrifice to live up to!

HOW LONG SHALL WE SIT IN
OUR PORTICOES PRACTICING
IDLE AND MUSTY VIRTUES,
WHICH ANY WORK WOULD
MAKE IMPERTINENT?

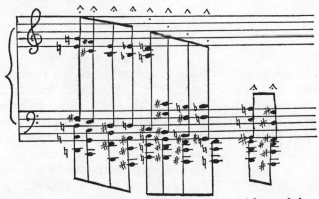

There is an attitude along this line evidenced by the Second String Quartet, by its lack of expressive marks, which I suspect is very deliberate.

The first two movements are called "DISCUSSION" and "ARGUMENT." It is not only the sound of the music which expresses this, but the very process of working on it. The quartet must explore it together, talk it through, make decisions about the relative importance of the parts, all the details, and how the details will be shaped into the whole. One thinks of the Schönberg chamber-works with their "Hauptstimme, Nebenstimme," etc. In Ives this determination of topmost, secondary parts, all the rest of this hierarchy of contrapuntal importance, is simply not present, any given successful solution being certainly not the only one possible.

With all this, Ives would not shrink from at times hurling Emerson's thunderbolts at your toughened ears, just inundating the mind with his big strong sound, totally overwhelming, as in some orchestral passages.

FOR I AM CONVINCED THAT I CANNOT EXAGGERATE ENOUGH EVEN TO LAY THE FOUNDATION FOR A TRUE EXPRESSION.

AND UNITY IS TOO GENERALLY CONCEIVED AS, OR TOO EASILY ACCEPTED AS, ANALOGOUS TO CUSTOM AND CUSTOM TO HABIT.

. . . AND VOTED THE WAY THEY ALWAYS DID.

The man is meditating in the midst of the vastness of Nature, and like Krishna in the Bagavad-Gita manifesting his ONE-ness as the sum of all reality, the Soul goes beyond "a place for everything and everything in its place" order . . . self given willingly a totality so complete that its details may—or must—seem different on each hearing.

THE ULTIMATE OF A CONCEPTION IS ITS VASTNESS.

IT IS A RIDICULOUS DEMAND WHICH ENGLAND AND AMERICA MAKE THAT YOU SHALL SPEAK SO THAT THEY CAN UNDERSTAND YOU. NEITHER MEN NOR TOADSTOOLS GROW SO.

Ives, in his "Essays Before a Sonata," reports that Carlyle, from the vantage point of European philosophy, found that Emerson did not quite cohere.

This seems to be to the point regarding much of the best art in America. The notion of ordering things merely by logical sequence is often expressly transcended.

HIS UNDERLYING PLAN OF
WORK SEEMS BASED ON THE
LARGE UNITY OF A SERIES
OF PARTICULAR ASPECTS OF
A SUBJECT, RATHER THAN ON
THE CONTINUITY OF ITS
EXPRESSION.

This new conception of form inheres in much music of the present day, and in other forms of art as well, the fruit of liberation from moment-to-moment causal necessities. This is the perfect intellectual key, in Ives's own words, to the world of sound he opened—as if direct perception of that sound were not revelation enough!

As thoughts surge to his mind, he fills the heavens with them, crowds them in, if necessary, but seldom arranges them along the ground first.

(This is also what I am doing in this paper.)

IF FOR EVERY THOUSAND-
DOLLAR PRIZE, A POTATO-
FIELD BE SUBSTITUTED, SO
THAT THESE CANDIDATES OF
CLIO CAN DIG A LITTLE IN
REAL LIFE.
. . . ART'S AIR MIGHT BE
A LITTLE CLEANER.
JUST LIKE A TOWN MEETING
—EVERY MAN FOR HIMSELF.
WONDERFUL HOW IT
CAME OUT.

Linked to "ideas of order" is seduction by surface polish. This seems to be a real contemporary American disease—from formica table-tops to the chrome lobby of the Time-Life Building.

Ives will have none of it. He addressed himself in the Essays to the question of expressive power, and finds a

vital distinction between *s*ubstance and *m*anner: that it is
this intentional lack of "slick" that has misled some into
thinking that Ives was an amateur. Lover! sure . . . certainly not a "pro." He knew the balance between "Love &
Power" and he knew how Thoreau knew it, as reflected
in his remark on the first page of this essay.

Just as Jackson Pollack said: as long as your mind stays
clear, you won't make a mess.

Here is an insight into the relation of macro- and micro-
cosmos that I wish some of the political reformers would
consider: With *true coherence*—total global interrelation,
the individual, the unit, may be *more,* rather than less, free.

OUR INVENTIONS ARE WONT   A FEAR OF FAILURE NEED
TO BE PRETTY TOYS, WHICH   KEEP NO ONE FROM THE
DISTRACT OUR ATTENTION   ATTEMPT.
FROM SERIOUS THINGS.
THEY ARE BUT
IMPROVED MEANS TO
UNIMPROVED ENDS.

The presence of those marches and hymns is *not* so
much evocation of the local scene (it isn't that at all) but
parts of the whole of reality, unlimited, multi-dimensioned.

It is Varèse's "Poème Electronique" which is the single
most developed consequence of such mental breadth—
evocative and expressive detail complementing a full array
of experiments-in-sound and innovations-in-form. The
true descendent is hardly Roy Harris or any of that folk-
song Americana bit, but rather the radios, recordings, random bits of everyday surrounding here-and-nows that become part of the compositions of musicians like John Cage.
No doubt this salutary influence has not yet come to the
end of its effect on us.

Anyway, 50 years before Ives, Thoreau himself described
what the music was going to sound like.

IF A MAN DOES NOT KEEP   . . . IN MUSIC, LIKE
PACE WITH HIS COMPANIONS,   OTHER TRUTHS . . . THERE

PERHAPS IT IS BECAUSE HE HEARS A DIFFERENT DRUMMER. LET HIM STEP TO THE MUSIC WHICH HE HEARS. . . . THE EVERLASTING VIGOR AND FERTILITY OF THE WORLD. WE CANNOT TOUCH A STRING OR MOVE A STOP BUT THE CHARMING MORAL TRANSFIXES US.

MUST ALWAYS REMAIN SOME FURTHER ELEMENT YET TO BE DISCLOSED.

Instead of no path to the front-yard gate in the Great Snow—no gate—no front yard—and no path to the civilized world.

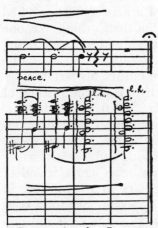

peace.

AND WE ARE ENABLED TO APPREHEND AT ALL WHAT IS SUBLIME AND NOBLE BY THE PERPETUAL INSTILLING AND DRENCHING OF THE REALITY THAT SURROUNDS US.

It remains for Ives to make the last deep remark:

THOREAU WAS A GREAT MUSICIAN, NOT BECAUSE HE PLAYED THE FLUTE BUT BECAUSE HE DID NOT HAVE TO GO TO BOSTON TO HEAR "THE SYMPHONY."

Panel Discussion on Thoreau

Walter Harding
Donald S. Harrington
Frederick T. McGill, Jr.

HARDING: IN THE CHAPTER FROM WALDEN, CALLED "READING," Thoreau says, "How many a man has dated a new era in his life from the reading of a book!" Thoreau had many prophetic things to say, but that, I think, was one of his most prophetic tenets. It is absolutely astounding the number of people who in the little more than one hundred years since Thoreau published his various writings dated a new era in their lives from the reading of various of his books: *Walden*, "Civil Disobedience," and many others, and this is one subject we will be discussing—the influence of Henry David Thoreau today.

Let me start with a rather striking and, I think, rather interesting example. Some forty years ago a friend of mine, who was at that time a clerk in a book store in Detroit, Michigan, was asked by a customer for a copy of *Walden*. As he took it down from the shelf and prepared to wrap it up, he leafed through the book and found it rather interesting. So the next Saturday, when he received his paycheck, he used part of it to buy himself a copy of *Walden*. He read it through and was so tremendously excited that the following Saturday night he bought another volume of Thoreau. On succeeding

82

Saturday nights he continued to buy copies of Thoreau's works until he had the complete collection. He then told his employer what he thought of book stores, Detroit in particular, and civilization in general, gave up his job, went up to the woods in Canada north of Lake Superior. He found himself his own little Walden Pond, five miles from the nearest neighbor, built his own cabin, and lived there for several years. On the inspiration of this experience, he wrote a volume of poetry, which, incidentally, won him a national prize.

On the strength of the prize he won, he came back to Detroit, looked up his old girl friend, proposed to her, married her, and took her back up to the woods north of Lake Superior. But after three months she told him he had to choose between her and beans. He chose her, came back to civilization, and, significantly, gave up writing poetry.

This is one striking example of the influence Henry Thoreau has had on individuals, but there are many others who have found Thoreau to be the person who has really changed their lives. He has had far more influence, I think, in our own generation than he did in his own.

With that as a start let me turn the discussion over to my partners here.

MCGILL: I think, Walt, that you will remember a story that Odell Shepard told us a good many years ago about a fellow recently graduated from Yale who did something like that—who found a hilltop in southern Massachusetts where he built a little cabin. He was persuaded after a year of living like Thoreau to come back because he belonged to a family that was important in one of Connecticut's great insurance companies. His grandfather had founded the company, his father was the

president, and of course he was expected to be kicked up
the ladder of success; after a year, he agreed that he
would go back in the family business. But over the years
succeeding he always bore in mind the fact that he was
sometime going back to his hilltop cabin, only he said
that the next time he was going to have a cow and a
wife—well, anyway, a cow. I think he is probably still
the president of the insurance company and probably
still keeps this in his mind.

HARRINGTON: You know, one of the interesting things,
Fred and Walt, is to see how these young people that
we've just been listening to here*—how well they caught
the fact that Thoreau was talking to them. In a sense,
I think he talks to every generation, but more to our
generation than to any other. Curiously, Thoreau had
a way of putting things so as to express an unconven-
tional thought in a way that would make people listen
and try to figure it out. Walter has spoken about the
fact that his book *Walden* has been a landmark book
in the lives of many people. One of the things he says
is: "Much is published, but little printed." This is one
of his famous aphorisms: "Much is published, but little
printed." It illustrates Thoreau's literary method. He
takes a common word and gives it a different twist, a
slightly different meaning. Of course, what he's saying
here is that with all of the flood of publishing, virtually
none of it is ever imprinted—none of it ever makes a
difference. *Walden* is one of those books that are printed.
I don't suppose we could say it's printed by looking at
our society, but we could say it's printed by listening
to the young people, by seeing the degree to which they
have thought from that piece, and one might say that

---

* The reference is to a series of interpretive readings and original
sketches about Thoreau performed by members of the college drama
society.

we have in the present generation perhaps the first generation really able to appreciate the spirit of Henry David Thoreau.

I want to ask Walter Harding a question: Walter, Thoreau lived in a small country town. I know that part of the country because I grew up there. As a boy, I often went swimming in Walden Pond, and I wandered through the fields and up along the Concord River that were his favorite places—by his favorite pond. I know how much it is still country. But how was it that a hundred and more years ago Henry Thoreau forecast so clearly what civilization was coming to?

HARDING: I think that's attributable to his perceptiveness, that he should speak of the necessity of simplifying our lives at a time when we now think of life as being very simple. He had the foresight to see what was going to happen with the trends that were developing, and it's the reason why he was not particularly appreciated in his own time—his fellow countrymen could not see the need for simplifying their lives. It was only when the directions which we were following in that time were carried to their logical conclusion that we've come to the difficulties that he predicted a hundred years ago. Over and over again I find people saying—and I know they're absolutely right on this—that they are astounded that *Walden* was written a hundred years ago. It seems as though it were a book written for today, not a century ago. A good example of its pertinence: LSD is a very contemporary topic, and William Braden's book* on this drug devotes a whole chapter to what he calls Yankee Hindus, and a section of Thoreau. He said Thoreau might have been an LSD addict, except that

---

* *The Private Sea: LSD and the Search for God* (Chicago: Quadrangle, 1967).

he didn't need LSD to turn himself on, and I think that's an important point.

MCGILL: You know, Walt, it seems to me that it was with a particular fitness that I came to this discussion of *Walden* by the route of the dashing commuter, and as I looked at that harried little man with the briefcase, in the circle which is stamped on the end of every car, I thought, this is why Thoreau has so much to say to us today. And I think that as we look back at his century and the part of the century that he occupied, we sometimes fail to realize that even in those days there were dashing commuters and people who were dashing at other activities, and from the point of view of a man like Thoreau, his generation was a lot more complicated than his father's and his grandfather's. The trend had gone far enough so that he could make comparisons, whereas as we look back it all seems pretty idyllic.

HARRINGTON: "Simplify!" he said. "Keep your accounts on your thumbnail!" You know, after I had read that, I introduced a regular column in my church newspaper that I called *Thumbnail Book Review:* I tried the discipline of getting a book review into three sentences.

HARDING: I wish some of the authors had done that!

HARRINGTON: I recommend it! You know, Thoreau also liked to try to say a great deal in a very few words. One might say that part of the difficulty in talking about Thoreau is that you're tempted to quote him all the time, so apt was his expression. His aphorisms are so striking and so . . . magnificent, they go so directly to the heart of the matter that it's very difficult not to quote. But, I think of a parallel, thinking of his contemporaneity and his brevity. One of the Thoreau poems that I fell in love with very early—and it's almost like a Haiku poem in its ability to say a great deal in a short space, and I think, again, the young people of our

age would respond to it—goes like this, if I can remember it:

> Love equals
> Swift and slow,
> And high and low,
> Racer and lame,
> The hunter and his game.

Isn't that a good definition?

HARDING: I'm glad, incidentally, that your mention of
Haiku gives me a lead-in; I went over to Japan a few
years ago to give a series of lectures there on Thoreau
at various universities and it amazed me how widely
known Thoreau is in Japan as in so many other foreign
countries. I found, for example, that in Tokyo you can
buy more different editions of Thoreau's works than
you can in New York City. And over and over again
the Japanese would say to me, "What did Thoreau read
of Zen Buddhism? He obviously understands it so much
better than most of us do." And when I said, "Well, he
simply hadn't read anything of Zen Buddhism; it wasn't
available in his day," they were astounded. Well this,
again, I think, shows the wide appeal—the wide interest
—this man has.

HARRINGTON: You know, "be" was one of his favorite words
—I'm just carrying out this same theme, Walter—which
makes him, though he was, I suppose, philosophically
an idealist and a transcendentalist, in his grasp of reality,
an existentialist. One of his favorite expressions was
that you should not be so much concerned with *doing;*
rather, he said, *"Be* thee." This is the contemporary
mood, and somehow, even back in that day when things
were so much simpler than they are today, he had
grasped the fact that this was the real challenge of life:
that doing, accumulating things, was all by-play, and

somehow apart from the real business of life, *being*. He said, you talk to me about business and being involved in business, but business is not *you*. What you really should be doing is living; *being* is the important thing.

HARDING: His famous couplet is most apropos:

My life has been the poem I would have writ,
But I could not both live and utter it,

except that he did both!

MCGILL: Don, you're speaking about his aphoristic or epigrammatic style; and, of course, he is distinguished by that, and it is true that he has dozens, maybe hundreds of quotable lines. If that were carried through a greater degree, perhaps, to an extreme, we'd have something like *Poor Richard's Almanack,* which is nothing but proverbs and/or epigrams. Fortunately, he knew where to stop and where to link his ideas together so that there was a continuity, as well as, let's say, a collection of smart generalizations. I'm reminded of something that he wrote in his notebook one night, after he had been to hear his friend, Ellery Channing, lecture in his local Lyceum. He said, it was a bushel of nuts, and then went on to explain to himself in his journal that he meant, of course, that each thought was a self-contained cartridge—I don't know how he said it; I know he said there was no sloping up or down to or from these ideas, that each one was given solely by itself and was self-sufficient. How much better the lecture would have been if there had been some connection between them—some bridging of the ideas; and he was conscious of this, you see, himself, and the necessity of doing it if he was going to be a really good writer and speaker, and I think he was a better one because he was aware of this. And perhaps he learned something from hearing the abuses of the aphoristic manner.

HARRINGTON: Fred, wasn't it true—didn't some of his critics suggest, that this was perhaps what might become his weakness?

MCGILL: Yes—oh yes—yes, indeed. Of course, Emerson did the same things, too. You could say his weakness is also his strength.

HARRINGTON: Wasn't there a strong moralizing aspect of Thoreau's view of the world? That is, there always seems to be a double point, as in that beautiful episode of his fishing for horned pout at night in Walden Pond, where he speaks of the line going down into the darkness of the water and his mind reaching out into the universe— the vastness of the universe—and he said, "I get a nibble on one line, and as I pull it in I realize I've got a bigger fish on the second line." And then he goes on to ruminate about this—about his having caught two fish on one hook, as it were, and speaks about the legislature's having said how many hooks you can have on a line. But, he said, most of those people know nothing of the Hook of hooks on which you can catch the pond itself. We wished the legislature might be the bait.

HARDING: Rather than the *de*-bate.

HARRINGTON: Another of his famous puns. Sometimes he carried his punning a little far.

HARDING: May I give the worst example, or are you going to?

HARRINGTON: No, you go ahead.

HARDING: That lovely line in *Walden* when he tells about coming back from Walden Pond one evening—or, leaving Walden Pond in the morning, I should say—and seeing one of the Concord farmers fishing on the pond. He returned in the evening and found the man still fishing, but the man had caught absolutely nothing. And he goes on to say that the man did not waste his day—that he was a member of that noble order of c-o-e-n-o-b-i-t-e-s. And if you look that word up in the dictionary, you'll discover it was an early Christian sect which practiced contemplation, which fits in appropriately, but when you pronounce the word, you see that he meant something entirely different because the word is pronounced "see, no bites."

We've been talking primarily about *Walden,* so far, and the simplification of life, but Thoreau has so many phases that I'd like to go over—at least temporarily—to another one. Don, I would like to ask you to say a word or two about civil disobedience, because that has so much influence and I know this has been a concern of your own as well as mine.

HARRINGTON: Yes, I'm very glad to do that. Of course Thoreau, in this essay on "Civil Disobedience," planted a seed, an idea that has had enormous consequences. Sometimes I like to use this as an illustration of the power of an idea. You ask the question, what is the most powerful thing in the world? Some people might say atomic energy, but then they'd have to say the idea $e = mc^2$ which released atomic energy. Perhaps the only thing that ultimately may tame atomic energy is another idea, this idea that Henry Thoreau gave utterance to in his essay on "Civil Disobedience," because it was that idea that Mahatma Gandhi used to set 400 million people free. It's just an idea, but the idea, having traveled to India and been used in India and made an example in India has come traveling back to Thoreau's own country to help set the Black people of this country free. Of course, there are real parallels between the situation today and the situation in Thoreau's time, especially with respect to the Mexican War and the involvement of our country in what Thoreau felt was an unjust war, which led to his essay on "Civil Disobedience" and his spending a night in jail. You know it's interesting, Walter and Fred, that the relevance stretches all the way from the field of man's need to maintain human quality, inner-ness, being-ness, to the most radical form of social action, civil disobedience.

HARDING: One of the things that has amazed me at the meetings of our Thoreau Society—all three of us happen to be members of the Thoreau Society which holds an annual meeting at Concord—is the tremendous variety of people who came to those meetings, each with his interest in Thoreau and each with a *different* interest in Thoreau. The Thoreau Society was originally started, I think, primarily because we were interested in writing about Thoreau and delving into his biography and criticism and things of that kind. But very quickly we found there were many, many other people who were anxious to join a group of people devoted to Thoreau, not because they had a scholarly interest, but because they had a deep personal interest. At some of our early meetings in Concord, when our meetings were small enough, we used to go around the group and ask each person, "How is it that you are interested enough in the writings of Henry Thoreau to travel 100 miles—500 miles, some of them even several thousand miles—to come to an annual meeting to discuss his works?" And the significant thing was, I think, that no two people ever got up and gave the same reason. Some people were interested in his nature writings, some in his style, some in his political ideas, some in his simplification of life—on and on and on. And the backgrounds of these people, too, ranging from clergymen to college professors—that's quite a range—and a kennel owner, a member of the Socialist Party, several business men—I've always thought it somewhat a paradox that the president of our society a few years ago was a stockbroker. I don't know what Henry would have thought of that, but a tremendously wide range of people find something significant, something pertinent, something—if I may be a little bit sentimental—something dear to them in the writings of Henry Thoreau.

MCGILL: Walt, in connection with the civil disobedience idea, does anyone ever suggest that the name Walden might be a very subversive anagram? If you rearrange the letters you get "end law."

HARDING: That's a pun that Henry would have liked.

MCGILL: Well, I've seen papers written on less than that. Of course, it's perfectly true that the pond was named long before Henry's time, but he could have picked out another pond—there were lots of them in Concord.

HARRINGTON: He liked White Pond, too. I can testify that the swimming is good at White Pond.

HARDING: I thought you were going to come up with an anagram on White Pond.

MCGILL: Don, I think one of the best talks I ever heard on Thoreau was one you gave in your church on the occasion of the centenary, and I remember that you took various railroad signs that you remembered from your boyhood in Waltham on the Fitchburg line and you ended with the mention of a sign that dated obviously back to a day when locomotives were real locomotives. And it said, "Look out for the engine!" and you applied this quite properly to some of the things that Thoreau has to say. I think it is the fact that there are more engines every year that we have to look out for that makes him so timely, and it is a mark of his prophetic powers, actually, that he saw this coming.

HARRINGTON: You have a feeling as you read *Walden* that he was almost obsessed with a kind of fear and of love for that engine that went by the corner of Walden Pond. Incidentally, I've walked along that track many times. Walking around the pond, you still come on the track; it cuts off a little corner of the pond where the old Boston and Maine, Fitchburg Line runs from Boston up to Fitchburg. Many times I've walked along, long before I read *Walden,* across the sleepers, the ties, under the rails, by that corner of the pond, and then taken off again on the path that winds around on the edge of the pond. He seemed to love that train at the same time that he disliked it and had forebodings about what it might portend.

HARDING: He certainly liked the whistle!

HARRINGTON: He loved the whistle; he speaks of the sound of the train coming, and the roar of it in the night. This brings us to another point, Fred and Walter: the incredible perceptiveness of this man to every aspect of sight and sound. One of the most interesting chapters in *Walden* is the one entitled "Sounds." How much more he heard than most people hear! Perhaps it's because there was more silence then. One was able to hear better than one can today.

Speaking of those railroad signs, the one at Waltham Highlands, where we lived, read, "Stop, Look, and Listen," and somebody had scrawled at the end, "and Live." Thoreau would have appreciated that phrase: Stop, look, listen; hear, see; this is what living *is*. Relate, enjoy life, don't let it get away from you. Up at the next crossing which is a very steep grade coming down from Prospect Hill, they had the sign that Fred McGill referred to, "Look out for the Engine!" I assume that was written mostly for drivers of horses that might well indeed have been scared by the engine coming around the corner.

HARDING: Your speaking a moment ago of his interest in sound brings up another whole facet of his appeal—the appeal that I suppose in the first place was the greatest, and that is the appeal—the interest in nature. Thoreau himself began one of his essays, "I want to speak a word for the wild." And he still is speaking a word for the wild. I've noticed that over and over again the various conservation campaigns today quote Thoreau in their publicity more than any other writer because he is still pertinent there. Just a week or two ago, one of the editors of *Newsweek* called me up—he said they were going to run an article on saving the redwoods in California, and he said, "Won't you find an appropriate quotation from Thoreau to use in our article?"

HARRINGTON: Does the Thoreau Society, or do you know if anyone, organizes opportunities to retrace some of the nature journeys of Thoreau? Wouldn't that be a good idea? Along the Concord and Merrimack Rivers, or perhaps down to Cape Cod?

HARDING: It's done completely on an individual basis, and I think that's the way Henry would approve. But it is surprising the number of people who consciously trace his steps, who have taken the trip along the Concord and Merrimack Rivers, or followed his footsteps on Cape Cod, or have canoed in the Allegash wilderness, or climbed Mount Wachusett or Mount Monadnock or Mount Washington. It's simply because he has described these areas so beautifully, so effectively, that they just urge people to follow his footsteps. I think it's also significant that virtually every place of this kind that he has written about has now become a State or a National Park. We have the National Seashore on Cape Cod; we have the National Forest around the White Mountains; we have a State Park at Mount Monadnock, another one at Mt. Wachusett; we have the National Recreation Area for the Allegash River. And I think it's primarily because Thoreau has written about these so effectively, so beautifully, that they've made people conscious of the fact that these areas must be saved for future generations. I think my only regret is that he didn't write about still more areas so that we'd have them saved, too.

MCGILL: Don, why don't we organize Thoreau Tours, Inc.,

and maybe we could make enough money to build a black road all the way along the shores of the Penebscot right up to the very beginnings of the river, and we could get thousands there every summer. Wouldn't that be a nice memorial?

HARRINGTON: With hot-dog stands in every park.

MCGILL: Oh yes, of course.

HARDING: There is, of course, a hot-dog stand at Walden Pond. I don't know how many people have told me that they've traveled great distances to see Walden Pond, and when they have gone to that little hot-dog stand, they said, "Could you tell me where Henry Thoreau lives," and the clerks there would scratch their heads and finally say, "Well, uh, I guess he doesn't live here any more—we, uh, we don't know him."

MCGILL: Walt, may I turn to something a little different? We all know that there are a lot of weird ideas about Thoreau that don't have very much basis in fact. You point out one or two, maybe more, in your book, *The Days of Henry Thoreau*. What do you think is the most prevalent misconception about Thoreau or about his stay at Walden?

HARDING: I think the most prevalent misconception is that Thoreau spent half his life at Walden Pond, and the other half in jail. Actually he spent two years at Walden Pond, and one night in jail. But he was able to describe those experiences so effectively that they have achieved a symbolical importance and have gone way out of proportion. I think another great misconception is that he was a misanthrope, a malcontent—that he was always criticizing society, when actually I feel it is exactly the opposite: that he was a person basically optimistic. If you look at all of his writings, all of his major writings, you'll notice that every single one ends on an optimistic note; as, for example, *Walden*'s ending with the statement, "The sun is but a morning star," the feeling that, if we, as human beings, only devote ourselves to it, we can develop a much better, a much greater life here on earth; and that "Civil Disobedience" ends with the statement that he can visualize a much more nearly perfect government if only we all work for it. He was not a pessimist. He was aware of the faults of our civilization and of our people and of himself. But he was concerned, not so much with those flaws *per se,* but rather with how to overcome them, and how to develop heaven here on earth.

MCGILL: I think of one other misconception, which, of course, is refuted by Thoreau's own words that we heard in the dramatic group performance before we came on here. This is the thought that he wants everybody to live the kind of life he lived, and he's advising us all to go out in the woods and build our huts. Of course he says that's not his intention—he wants us to live our own lives, but think through what we really want to do.

HARRINGTON: He had that marvelous tolerance for differences. I think if there's any message that some of us need to take to heart in this age of the little boxes, it is really that we don't all have to be alike. Thoreau was quite content to be a maker of pencils and do an occasional surveying job to get his money, and to spend the rest of his time living, thinking, and writing. A good many people might look down on a maker of pencils. I mean that this, after all, is a rather routine job. He was content to do a routine job. He was a surveyor, which line of work isn't too difficult to learn. Sometimes he complained, though, that the surveying spoiled his appreciation on some of his walks, because, he said, he knew where the stakes were which marked out the property lines.

This does bring up another question, Fred. What a curious blend of the practical and, you might almost say, mystical! He would say, Don't pay so much attention to these mundane things, and then keep an accurate record of everything he spent while he was at Walden. He would talk about the beauty of the pond, and then drop a line down and measure it, so that he would have a precise statement of how deep it was at every spot. This combination of the aesthetic and practical is almost paradoxical.

MCGILL: He loved paradox, and that's one of the things he recognized in himself as sometimes a failing; like his exaggeration, which he realized also was a tendency that he had to keep on a leash, so to speak.

HARRINGTON: Some of these young people are interested in the field of writing. Perhaps you two professors could tell us, what does the ability to sense a paradox in common things have to contribute to one's writing ability and style? I'll make it a little more concrete. I came across in one of the journals this rather impressive statement. And the reason I cite it is that I think we're coming to a new appreciation of the fact that the way we get at the deepest truth is often through the mythological statement of it. Thoreau had the equivalent of this; he had the ability to see a deep truth shining through a commonplace event—or somewhere behind it or just a hint of it in it.

This is what he wrote in his journal of 1851: "My fact shall be falsehoods to the common sense. I would so state facts that they shall be significant—shall be myths, or mythologics." I shall so state facts that they shall be myths or mythologics. Well, somehow or other, he had found a way to catch this deeper dimension into a commonplace statement, and maybe this is why we are so appreciative of him today. He had caught something that was universal and immortal, and we recognize it—we recognize ourselves in the reflection of it.

HARDING: Thoreau said that he used to keep two different notebooks; one to jot down facts, and one to jot down poetry, and he often found he didn't know which book he put something in. And this is so true of his own writings; you don't know whether to call it facts or poetry—it does have this exact idea.

MCGILL: So often the statements that we consider paradoxical have two truths in them. They seem to be at war with each other, and yet either one by itself can be defended. It's like what Robert Frost does in a poem like "The Tuft of Flowers." You remember. Men work together, whether they work together or apart. He has one proposition in the beginning of the poem, and then the opposite later on.

HARRINGTON: And they're both true!

MCGILL: Yes, they're both true. And "Good Fences Make Good Neighbors." I mean, you could make a case for that, but he makes it clear that it's the other side that he prefers in his poem "Mending Wall." You could make a good poem with either one as its climax.

HARRINGTON: There is a real parallel between Frost and Thoreau. They used the same method.

MCGILL: Very much.

HARRINGTON: It's rare for Frost to write a poem without a double point.

MCGILL: Well, isn't it a good deal like the basic conflict in a good story? There is no narrative that's any good unless there's some fight going on and you want to see how it comes out. And in a way these ideas that say this are like two characters at war with one another, and we want to see which one comes out on top. But they are both respectable antagonists, each one a fit match for the other.

HARRINGTON: And so clever is he with words that sometimes he uses the same word. I remember, for example, another one of his famous sayings, and I think it was Carlyle who told him he should travel and see the world, that it would enrich his thought, his life, and his writings. He is supposed to have replied, "I have traveled a good deal in Concord." Obviously he's taken this word "travel" and given it a twist which makes it mean almost the opposite of what Carlyle meant when he used it. This gift for being able to bring out a different meaning and make you stop and think about it, is, I think, his greatest gift. Anyone who will pick up *Walden* and give himself two minutes I guarantee will keep on reading it.

HARDING: I'd like to go back to a question you asked a few minutes ago, Fred. You spoke about the misconceptions, and I think one of the most prevalent is that he was lazy. I suppose this stems from the statement he made in his commencement address when he graduated from Harvard, that he hoped the Biblical directive would be reversed and that, instead of having six days of work and resting the seventh, we should have one day of work and rest six. And how he applied that in his own life when he used to boast that he worked six weeks a year and then rested the rest! But what he spoke of as rest wasn't rest at all; it was hard work. And if anyone thinks that Henry Thoreau was lazy, I'd like to point out that at the time of his death at the age of forty-four, he left more than two million words of some of the best prose we have in our language, and for those of you who have had to turn in freshman papers of a thousand words, stop to think what it would be to write two million words of deathless prose.

HARRINGTON: I think we've come to the end of the time, Walter. I remember one of the sentences in one of his journals. He said, "I spent yesterday in New York. I didn't come across one real live person." Toward the end of *Walden,* he says we tolerate an incredible dullness. He's asking us to live. I wonder if any generation ever needed more that admonishment, his exhortation.

HARDING: And I wonder if there is any man who is more alive than Henry Thoreau. In closing I'd like to go to a far distant point of the universe, all the way to Russia. About 1900, Leo Tolstoy somehow ran across the writings of Thoreau and became so excited about them that he wrote a letter that he sent to what was then our leading periodical, the *North American Review,* an article which he entitled, "A Letter to the American People." In it he said, "Why don't you Americans stop paying attention to your admirals, your generals, your millionaires, and pay attention to one of the most important writers you have—Henry David Thoreau."

Thoreau and Poetry

Muriel Rukeyser

THOREAU, WHOM WE COME TO HONOR, SPEAKS TO US TODAY.
You have been hearing, seeing the traces of Thoreau in
our own time. I imagine much of what I am going to
say to you may be recapitulation. But I want to re-
capitulate for you, from this place where I stand, the effort
of a person, in conscious life, to make something that
can flash again and again with an integral moment in
its flashing. Thoreau speaks to us of the great difficulty
of our own lives to pull themselves into that integrity,
speaks in that flash of reality which is the present moment
always, which is now, which is the only real, and of which
Thoreau was deeply conscious.

I do not know how you have been hearing about him.
You have heard from people whose lives are deep in his
work and life. Professor Harding, whose work one must
know to find this, is here, and Mr. Feinberg, whose work
has helped to make this possible, and Carl Bode, who made
the poems available and remade the edition of the poems.
Many people, many people living and dead—I think of
Matthiessen, whom I knew and who reached Thoreau
from where *he* lived in a way that comes into this deeply.
The process goes back; it goes back to Thoreau's own
recognition of the young Whitman. He came not only to
the poems but to Brooklyn; he came here—he speaks of

103

the beach at Rockaway—he lived at Staten Island; he came
to Emerson: "The American Scholar" was the address
that he heard while he was still at college. And before
that, we reach what he reached—the people he reached
and their work. I name Goethe, Coleridge, Thomas
Browne, because it is these currents that make the process.
And it is not simple; it is not a man walking in the woods,
as we say "a man walking in the woods." Because every
word of Thoreau's would have to be gone to, and gone
to according to your own life, according to the difficulties,
the parts of one's self that one dislikes, the parts of one's
self that won't fit in with all the rest, except with extraordinary and skilled, disciplined, wild effort. Because he was
aware, he treated openly the difficulties that he had, the
difficulties that are open to us all, in his illness—that is,
T.B. How to live with it? The difficulty in facing his own
body, which he felt awkward with; the difficulty visible
in even a drawing of Thoreau. You can see a lot of it.

There are discrepancies. These are his materials. There
are discrepancies in what I have to deal with, with you
today, in the way the poems are and in what he believed
poetry must be. A lot of this does not "match"; and it is
a fact of the not matching which is of value to us, and
is deep in this curious man who was like us in that he
didn't "match."

How to live with that; how to make a life in this world!

I want to come to "In wildness is the preservation of
the world." You can't come to that without his saying
the suburban, very suburban remark that we all know:
"I wish my neighbors were wilder," he said. It's that he
didn't have enough of it in himself—he wanted it. He
didn't have it around him—he wanted it. He didn't have
it in his country—he wanted it. It is the wish, it is the
desire, that doesn't match what one sees, this desire of
which he is the great artist and saint. And if this leads
to the life at Walden, if this leads to civil disobedience,

if this leads to the poems, to poetry, if this leads to pieces of a book with titles like "Economy," "Solitude," "Walking," what is this, what does it say to us?

It is not the hermit saint, unified, integrated, finding regularity of verse, making the best pencils that anybody could make at that time, living in friendship with Emerson, living in love so that we are twin stars, no longer planets. It is the man frustrated in friendship, irritating beyond belief; frustrated in love, both his brother and himself turned down by the woman they loved. In love with his own people who were, finally, in Civil War, the culmination of the struggle during his lifetime and long before.

He faces the moment with everything that does not match, that does not fit, and sees this meeting as the potential.

This potential has to be dealt with if one is dealing with reality.

Thoreau wanted to deal with reality. More than walking on the earth and mud and muck; although he would have that; he said he must have that. He said he would find the reality, the rocks, underneath so that you could say, "This is it," of the reality you found.

I want to come to him through poems, and even the people who speak most fully and with most understanding about his poems are likely to say something disparaging in the next moment. Even the people who believe they love his poems will say something that pulls most of it back right after and will take you to his prose. I say there is a huge distinction, even in the rhythms—the rhythms of the prose, say, are wilder than the rhythms of the poems, which are, if you will excuse me, suburban in relation to the forest of the prose. Emerson said that these poems were the best poems to come out of our American forest. But they come out of many things. They come out of the pressure on Thoreau to be a pastoral poet. This was a pastoral strip made in the attempt to make a civilized strip of America. He was reaching for something beyond him as we reach for something beyond us. And it is *that* that did the work on him; it is *that* kind of poet that he is. He will say what he loves in prose, and it's a curious person whom he loves, and he says this of his maxims, "They are not philosophy but poetry." This is not Goethe; this is not Coleridge; this is Raleigh, Sir Walter Raleigh, and this is one of the ways in which I come to Thoreau.

Raleigh longed for the new world. Raleigh! How could Thoreau have anything in common with Raleigh, a marvelous silver and crimson man, the man whose arrogance is deep of his downfall; with the pearls in his ears; with the fortune spent on his clothing; with a fortune thrown away as a gesture that every child knows as a story—he threw his cloak down before Queen Elizabeth when she came to a plashy place. Raleigh was a sea-going boy, a west-country boy. His family were Grenvilles and Gilberts. He wanted the new world. He wanted these unknown forests, the unknown shores. "Rockaway," says Thoreau. We know Rockaway. It is something quite different by now. It is the coast of the new world, stretching beyond a possible Northwest Passage, stretching beyond the people —unknown people. Red men—what's that? Infinite riches— what's that? Wildness—what's that?

Raleigh never got there. Raleigh was not allowed to leave. Queen Elizabeth would not let him leave. She kept him as Captain of the Guard, all sparkling, outside the court chamber. But young Hariot is how I come to Raleigh, young Thomas Hariot,* a scientist, the kind of scientist that we have not even imagined yet, because we say men are specialized; a man makes pencils—all right, he is a pencil-maker; a man lives by the side of water, whether it is a pond or the sea—all right, he is a fisherman.

---

* Muriel Rukeyser, *The Traces of Thomas Hariot* (New York: Random House, 1970).

Now Hariot was one of the people who had not specialized. Hariot was the young scientist who was the explorer who *did* come here. It is as if we had trained one of our astronauts, one of our poets, one of our scientists, that is, to be an astronaut, to go to the moon, to go wherever, and to write the report—chart it—write whatever it is, tell us. Not describe—we call it describe—*not* describe. Give us an experience so that we have an experience that lets us understand what it feels like to be a man thinking these things.*

Raleigh sent the expedition out—this was 1585—it is over three hundred years before Thoreau was doing all this and Raleigh stayed in England. But Raleigh, in what he wrote, in what he caused people to do, speaks to Thoreau. Thoreau says of the Raleigh writing—I think I can say it without having it before me—says, "It is a branch of greenness laid across the page. It is as if a green bough were laid across the page."

And Raleigh, this man so outwardly different, with so many complexities in his nature, with that pride, with that ability to incorporate his body into his thinking, spoke to Thoreau and formed many of the wild and fresh and difficult ideas of a new world so that Thoreau will say of the difficulties, of the things one reaches for (and this is when he is writing about Raleigh) , "What is truth? That which we know not. What is beauty? That which we see not. What is heroism? That which we are not."

It is *that* kind of man who is able to deal with the unknown, with that which he is not, as part of himself. This is how one climbs. This is how Thoreau climbed. This is how we come to what he wanted poems to be. There are two distinct things here, and he allows for both: what he wants them to be and what he makes.

This is what he says he wants poems to be (he is speaking of Raleigh's poems) : "They are in some respects more

---

* Cf. R. G. Collingwood, *Principles of Art* (New York: Oxford, 1938) .

trustworthy testimonials to his character than state papers or traditions. For poetry is a piece of very private history which unostentatiously lets us into the secret of a man's life, and is to the reader what the eye is to the beholder, the characteristic feature which cannot be distorted or made to deceive." We are told this about the camera, "which cannot be distorted or made to deceive," and we all know pictures, we all know snapshots, movies. We know what the camera cannot do. But this is the eye, and this is poetry. It is a way that poetry is *not* spoken of very often. "The characteristic feature which cannot be distorted or made to deceive. Poetry is always impartial and unbiased evidence. The whole life of a man may safely be referred to a few deep experiences." It is in this way that Thoreau speaks to us.

Is that true? Is that true for you? That the whole of your life can be referred to a few deep experiences? Thoreau doesn't use the word "safely" very often. He is not interested in safety except in this line just quoted. But safely, surely! Think of your main deep experiences. They are the expressive things. Even if you think of them as "happening to" you, they are the ways in which you have expressed yourself. That is what Thoreau gives us in his view of poetry and in his poems—a momentary flash in which, if a man prepares for it, a life can be expressed to other lives.

Now he does not say, although we know from his life and what he has written and his way of living, he does not speak very much of the discipline that goes into it. He speaks of it obliquely . . . not obliquely at all, perfectly straight to it. He will tell us, detail by detail, of what he has observed—that is, what has acted on him. He will say what he cannot tolerate in the society around him, and what he is willing to do to place his body and his life at the situations he cannot tolerate.

His poems can be taken as evidence of this. I would like to quote a few of these poems to you.

"I am a Parcel of Vain Strivings Tied," we are given as the title of this. It is the first line of the poem. These poems have all been taken from among the prose—most of them—jottings, and they should be read that way, because this is a life in writing in which the relationship between prose and poetry is acknowledged openly, always:

I am a parcel of vain strivings tied
By a chance bond together,
Dangling this way and that, their links
Were made so loose and wide,
Methinks,
For milder weather.

A bunch of violets without their roots,
And sorrel intermixed,
Encircled by a wisp of straw
Once coiled about their shoots,
The law
By which I'm fixed.

A nosegay which Time clutched from out
Those fair Elysian fields,
With weeds and broken stems, in haste,
Doth make the rabble rout
That waste
The day he yields.

And here I bloom for a short hour unseen,
Drinking my juices up,
With no root in the land
To keep my branches green,
But stand
In a bare cup.

The next poem is called "The Thaw":

I saw the civil sun drying earth's tears—
Her tears of joy that only faster flowed,

Fain would I stretch me by the highway side,
To thaw and trickle with the melting snow,
That mingled soul and body with the tide,
I too may through the pores of nature flow.

But I alas nor trickle can nor fume,
One jot to forward the great work of Time,
'Tis mine to hearken while these ply the loom,
So shall my silence with their music chime.

And with the sorrow and discrepancy that goes into those, comes also a man's own idea of hell. This is Thoreau:

No earnest work that will expand the frame,
And give a soundness to the muscles too?
How ye do waste your time!
Pray make it worth the while to live,
Or worth the while to die.
Show us great actions piled on high,
Tasking our utmost strength touching the sky,
As if we lived in a mountainous country.
    Hell were not quite so hard to bear
If one were honored with its hottest place.
And did ye fear ye should spoil Hell
By making it sublime?

Two more. This is called "Loves Invalides". . . . This is the other side. These are the other side, if you like, of Thoreau, the things—the material—out of which he made, finally, his simplicities. This is called, from its first line, "Loves Invalides are not those of Common Wars":

Loves invalides are not those of common wars
    More than its scars—
They are not disabled for a higher love
    But taught to look above.

With erring men I have small affair
Though they can do some harm and do not care.
It is a part of them which I can not commend
A part of them that never was my friend.

And this is a very short one called "I Was Made Erect
and Lone":

    I was made erect and lone
    And within me is the bone
    Still my vision will be clear
    Still my life will not be drear
    To the center all is near
    Where I sit there is my throne
    If age choose to sit apart
    If age choose give me the start
    Take the sap and leave the heart.

He said in his journal on March 25th, a Friday, 1842:
"Great persons are not soon learned, not even their out-
lines, but they change like the mountains and the horizon
as we ride along." His greatness comes reflected to us from
what he did and what he thought. We have this evidence:
he spoke for one's body and one's thoughts, what one
writes, one's thoughts or what one lives out in action. This
action, as you know, became the great river of disobedience
as a means to front *the other* in life, *the other* in society.

Disobedience is of course only a negative way of putting
it. The positive way is the fronting: the fronting of life,
with hostility reduced all the way down, since one knows

what hostility makes in another person. One knows what kind of animal one is and how one responds to hostility. One knows what it whips up in oneself.

I know it is only the violent person who understands nonviolence—who has to wake up every morning and be nonviolent for one more day. It is only the person who knows what it is to be irritating, to be hostile, who knows what the long physical battle is to put down—not put down, but to deal with hostility in oneself, to use all the parts of it which are usable, because there *are* ways to use war in oneself.

One man can make art of this. This is one of the ways of art, to use the warlike, to use the ways of active struggle. It can be shown; it can be given to other people; it can be given in art.

But in the hostilities, in such a war as Vietnam in which the imagination has not yet been released to solve it—it is a political action like the political actions of which Thoreau wrote.

We have the qualities in ourselves to deal with political struggle. The ways which are taken as being hysterical, which are the civilized ways of dealing with political struggle, such as demonstration, speaking, putting your life where your opinions are—these are taken as hysterical and childlike. It is perfectly apparent what is hysterical and childlike. Not childlike, because it is not what children do. It is what wild hostility in oneself does, undealt with, not met with the imagination as Thoreau insisted on meeting it. And simply not paying a tax, walking into jail, is one of the ways to deal with it, so that one prepares oneself for jail. As the California poet Marie Welch said, we would be better off if we did our work improving the conditions of jails, because many of us may go there.

Thoreau saw the life of a poet as part of these ways of responding. And those of you who are students know it in yourselves. You are told always that your student time

is a preparing for life—to be something else, to live in
some other way. We know the ways of the phases of life,
and how in each phase of a man's life he becomes something different. In nature, in a way, as ice, in nature, becomes water—becomes steam, and is all one's life. Thoreau will laugh at some of the preparations. And you
know how many times in life you have been told to hold
still; don't let your real feelings come into this—you are
preparing for another part of life. Thoreau says that "this
spending of the best part of one's life earning money in
order to enjoy a questionable liberty during the least
valuable part of it reminds me of the Englishman who
went to India to make a fortune first, in order that he
might return to England and live the life of a poet. He
should have gone up garret at once."

Here is another poem:—I read you poems; Thoreau
wrote poems, and he said that the real poem is what the
poet himself has become. Now, he would argue the other
way, too, and say, when you have the poem you don't
need the biography. He will give you both sides; he will
give you all the discrepancies. But he has said, among the
discrepancies, the real poem is what the poet himself has
become.

This poem was written and then lengthened. I am
going to present it to you in its shorter form, which I love.
It is the poem called "Wachusett." This is as it is in the
journals:

> But special I remember thee,
> Wachusett, who like me
> Standest alone without society.
> Thy far blue eye,
> A remnant of the sky,
> Seen through the clearing or the gorge,
> Or from the windows of the forge,
> Doth leaven all it passes by.

Nothing is true
But stands 'tween me and you,
Thou western pioneer,
Who know'st not shame nor fear,
By venturous spirit driven
Under the eaves of heaven;
And canst expand thee there,
And breathe enough of air?

And this quatrain:

I've searched my faculties around
To learn why life to me was lent
I will attend his faintest sound
And then declare to man what God hath meant.

And also this poem. I'd like to read the last lines first
and then go back to the beginning, because the strength
of what he meant deeply is in small, in seed, in these
last lines:

Implacable is Love,—
Foes may be bought or teased
From their hostile intent,
But he goes unappeased
Who is on kindness bent.

It starts with its opposite, of course. It's called, from its
first line, "Let Such Pure Hate Still Underprop," and the
epigraph is "Friends, Romans, Countrymen, and Lovers":

Let such pure hate still underprop
Our love, that we may be
Each other's conscience,
And have our sympathy
Mainly from thence.

We'll one another treat like gods,
And all the faith we have
In virtue and in truth, bestow
On either, and suspicion leave
To gods below.

Two solitary stars,—
Unmeasured systems far
Between us roll,
But by our conscious light we are
Determined to one pole.

What need confound the sphere,—
Love can afford to wait.
For it no hour's too late
That witnesseth one duty's end,
Or to another doth beginning lend.

It will subserve no use,
More than the tints of flowers,
Only the independent guest
Frequents its bowers,
Inherits its bequest.

No speech though kind has it,
But kinder silence doles
Unto its mates,
By night consoles,
By day congratulates.

What saith the tongue to tongue?
What heareth ear of ear?
By the decrees of fate
From year to year,
Does it communicate.

and now I'm jumping to the end:

> There's nothing in the world I know
> That can escape from love,
> For every depth it goes below,
> And every height above.
> It waits as waits the sky,
> Until the clouds go by,
> Yet shines serenely on
> With an eternal day,
> Alike when they are gone,
> And when they stay.
>
> Implacable is Love,—
> Foes may be bought or teased
> From their hostile intent,
> But he goes unappeased
> Who is on kindness bent.

I want to stop with these poems, but I want to leave you also with the moment that follows, "In wildness is the preservation of the world." They don't quote that passage. They stick to the first sentence as if it were a maxim. But it is part of something; and to prepare for that, something else that he said in *Walden*: "We need to witness our limits transgressed and see some light pasturing freely where ours never wander." And then to the great statement on wildness, which comes from the man he is to the wildness which we all imagine, "In wildness is the preservation of the world. Every tree sends its fibers forth in search of the wild."

Thoreau and India

Kamala Bhatia

THOREAU'S MYSTICISM HAS A QUALITY WHICH DRAWS THE attention and admiration of the people of India. An analysis of his mysticism as revealed in his works reveals its closeness to Indian thought through the ages.

Perhaps the most important quality that one associates with the true mystic is his life and character. When he was asked by someone what was man's original purpose and destiny, Thoreau replied that he was unable to answer such a question, but added: "The noblest man is, methinks, that knows and by his life suggests the most about these things." Thoreau believed that living is far more important than "knowledge" itself. In this he agreed fundamentally with all mystics. The *Upanishads* declare that liberation is not the result of the knowledge of Atman, but that man becomes imbued with knowledge since he lives in such a way that "ordinary minds cannot understand his actions, life, or movements, any more than a dreaming man can see the world of those who are awake." In other words, because of his special character, the mystic becomes one with what he knows and acts accordingly, not only after the experience but before as well. Thoreau's whole life was a quest for the heroic or the perfection of self-realization. One can find in his college essays his opposition to conformity, to polite society, to formal religion, in his quest for perfect self-realization. In his essay

"The Service," Thoreau deals with the absolute integrity of man in relation to life. In *Walden* he replied to Plotinus's statement that the mystic gives up "power, strength, wealth, beauty and science because he has found something better, a vision of truth, surpassing anything that temporal life has to offer."

Thoreau, we see, was obsessed with the idea of heroism, and mystical genius. We may ask how does a hero or mystical genius differ from an ordinary man?

One of the primary qualities of such a mystical genius would be his highly developed spiritual awareness. He feels dissatisfied with the world as it appears and perceives that there is a better world which can be apprehended here and now. To entertain this belief is the beginning of a mystical life, for it necessitates an enquiring and dissatisfied soul in order to turn his back on the practical world, because it is the apparent and illusory world that prevents him from experiencing the real. The *Upanishads* hold as their first principle the theory that the essence of things is not given in the objects as they present themselves in space and time, and give it the name *Maya* or illusion:

> Children pursue outer pleasures and fall into the net of widespread death; but calm souls having known what is unshakeable Immortality do not covet any uncertain thing in the world.

Thoreau was conversant with the Indian idea of *Maya*, and this is evident from this passage in *The Dial*:

> Whatever is on earth is the resemblance and shadow of something that is in the sphere. While the resplendent thing remaineth in good condition, it is well also with its shadow. When that resplendent thing removeth far from its shadow, life removeth to a distance. . . . The perfect seeth unity in multiplicity and multiplicity in unity.

Thoreau said that he could do the meanest work ever to satisfy the demands of "Hindoo Penance" to make this reality, so that he could experience the "unity" of timeless eternity. He had a spiritual awareness of Nature; the whole course of Nature with its laws and methods, its constant regularity, beauty, and symmetry, evoked his worship and admiration of the Creator from whom all proceeds. In his theology of nature, in the flux or ebb and flow, God was always present. For Thoreau, the apparent world of shadows, an integral part of Being, was not to be neglected while attempting to perceive the real world of reality:

> Both a conscious and unconscious life are good. Neither is good exclusively, for both have the same source. . . . Indeed it is obeying the suggestions of a higher light within you that you escape from yourself and in the transit, as it were, see with the unworn side of your eye, travel totally new paths.

To reach the goal of spiritual reality, the true mystic has to get to the very center of his being; there has to be a reorientation, an ecstasy, an extension of being.

Transcendentalism as a religious-philosophical movement had, as one of its aims, the moral regeneration of man, an extension of being; but with Thoreau it became not only an aim but a living reality.

Sri Aurobindo Ghose, one of India's great mystics and philosophers, expressed essentially the same sentiments as Thoreau:

> To become ourselves is the one thing to be done; but the true ourselves is that which is within us, and to exceed our outer self of body, life and mind is the condition for this highest being, which is our true and divine being.

To Thoreau, spiritual realization produced harmony with all existence. He wrote in his journal:

The thinker is he who is serene and self possessed. . . . He who can deal with his thoughts as a material . . . building them into poems which future generations will delight. . . . He is the man of energy in whom subtle and poetic thoughts are bred.

Like the Indian poets and mystics, Thoreau loved nature and was so much in harmony with it that he could feel the very pulse beating through nature. That the poet was universally related and was the spokesman of the divine reality within manifested itself in Thoreau's unique description of morning as the poets' hour:

> Methinks that Time has reached his prime
> Eternity is the flower
> And this the faint confused chime,
> That ushers in the sacred hour.

The poet, then, utilized his faculties and became the exposition of the divine Mind. He "sometimes tastes the genuine nectar and ambrosia of the gods and lives a divine life." The poet was in harmony with the divine will, and any experiences that he had were manifestations of the divine "aura." In the *Week,* he wrote: "Poetry is the mysticism of mankind," and hence, for Thoreau, the mightiest experience of which man is capable was the special province of the poet. Rabindranath Tagore expresses the same idea when he writes: "The progress of our Soul is like a perfect poem. It has an infinite idea which once realized makes all movements full of meaning and joy."

Although all mystics have not been poets and all poets have not been mystics, the mystic has in general loved to tell mankind of his explorations into the nature of the Divine. Jacob Boehme, Meister Eckhart, Thomas à Kempis, St. Augustine, Plotinus, Jonathan Edwards in the West, and in India the singers of the *Upanishads,* the

Bhagavad Gita, Sankara, Ramayana, Kabir, Aurobindo
Ghose, Rabindranath Tagore, Mahatma Gandhi all have
felt a compelling need to express the results of the divine
life. One knows that the sanctity of their respective lives
was their foremost concern, not their written account of
the divine life. So it is with Thoreau, and in this regard
he differed from Emerson, whose mysticism (if it may be
called that) was of a utilitarian type. In fact, for Thoreau,
spiritual awareness preceded and was more important than
the idea expressed.

A complex aspect of Thoreau's concept of spiritual
reality and particularly his understanding of the creativity
of man and the world, was his interest in the spiritual
and the wild: both are an integral part of his mystical
life-view. In *Walden* he writes:

> The wildest scenes had become unaccountably familiar. I
> found in myself, and still find an instinct toward a higher,
> or as it is named, spiritual life as do most men, and another
> toward a primitive rank and savage one, and I reverence
> them both.

According to him wild life is not wild by ordinary
standards, but is pure and innocent, just as spiritual life
is pure and innocent. Alan Watts has written that all
mythology looks back nostalgically to an age when man
was still in a pristine state of divinity. Adam and Eve in
the Garden of Eden exemplify the "golden age." The
golden age, according to Alan Watts, is a "natural state
of primitivity and infancy wherein consciousness is so
fascinated and absorbed in extremes that it does not reflect
upon itself."

One can see that this concept of being approximates
the mystical state of "Is-ness" of Eckhart and "Such-ness"
of Zen Buddhism and Liberation in Brahminism. This
subtle doctrine enables us to understand Thoreau's wish:

"I look back to those fresh but now remote hours as to the dawn of time, when a solid blooming health reigned and every deed was simple and heroic."

The wild represented a harmony between "natural man" and the external world. Hence, the goal of the spiritual for Thoreau was to go beyond appearances and come to the realization of spirit or universal will in and behind nature. This was Sri Aurobindo's idea also.

A corollary to all these facts which Thoreau divines and which are inherent in his mysticism was delight in all existence. In his joyous affirmation of the principle of creation, one comes to an important but often ignored or misunderstood aspect of Thoreau. His affinity with creation is in reality the very heart of his spiritual awareness. Thoreau's attitude toward creation reflects the Indian Brahmanic principle of *Anand* or Bliss, the delight in existence. According to N. A. Nikam, Bliss is the creative principle whereby the original solitariness and fear of the Person (spirit) behind creation is overcome by Himself, by his act in creating the world. Creation is a sharing of the delight of existence.

Thoreau also held, as all mystics hold, that the physical senses in themselves were not modes of mystical apprehension. He agreed that to become one with Brahma, according to the *Bhagavad Gita,* the seer turned away from sound and other objects of sense and cast aside attraction and diversion. The *Upanishads* too cautioned against the use of the senses in apprehending Self. Brahma is not grasped by the eye or by speech or by other senses.

Thoreau occasionally gave a lucid view of the oneness he experienced, as when he wrote: "In some fortunate moment, the voice of eternal wisdom reaches me, in the strain of the sparrow, and liberates me, whets and clarifies my senses, makes me a competent witness."

From this it is clear that Thoreau experienced an expansion of being, an ecstasy which led to a vision of "eternal wisdom"—all from clarified senses.

Sri Aurobindo, the Indian mystic, experienced ecstasies similar to Thoreau's. He describes that those who entered the power of a more dynamic life experienced "an enlargement, a rush of new experience, a great vision. . . . It was a joy of being which is larger and richer than any delight in existence that the outer vital man on a surface mentality can gain by this dynamic vital force and activity or subtlety and expansion of the mental existence."

This is what Aurobindo experienced as *Anand*—the delight in existence. One can explain more fully Thoreau's experiences of this nature and of his expansion of being into a vision that transcends the normal senses by turning to an analysis that Thoreau himself gave in the *Week*. Here he differentiates the several modes of apprehension by the senses: "I perceive in the common traits of my thoughts a natural and uninterrupted sequence, each implying the next, or if interruption occurs, it is occasioned by a new object being presented to my senses." He describes the completely different perception as:

But a steep and sudden, and by these means unaccountable transition, is that from a comparatively narrow and partial, what is called commonsense, view of things to an infinitely expanded and liberating one, from seeing things as men describe them, to seeing them as men cannot describe them.

The "purely sensuous life," then, was potentially for Thoreau a mode of mystical prehension for all creation, all existence. The *Svetasvatara Upanishad* assured that the pure, sensuous life is a means of approaching the Inner Reality, in the following words:

To realise God, first control the outgoing sense and harness the mind. Then meditate upon the light in the heart of fire—

meditate, that is, upon pure consciousness of the intellect. Thus the Self, the Inner Reality, may be seen behind appearances and with the help of the mind and the intellect, keep the senses from attaching themselves to objects of pleasure. They will then be purified by the light of the Inner Reality, and that light will be revealed.

Not only do these particular lines from the *Upanishad* testify to the efficacy of the purified senses as a means of mystical apprehension, but the writings of Eckhart, too, validate the same doctrine.

Of his senses, one may say that rarely has there been a person so sensitive to *sound* as Thoreau was. His sense of hearing had the power of intensifying his mystical perception. Hearing also had the power to change time to eternal morning, the poets' hour. Sound, however, was not the ultimate experience of mystical perception, for it acted as a handmaiden to Silence. "Silence is when we hear inwardly, sound when we hear outwardly." Simple sounds could relate him to God. In his journal, Thoreau tried to delineate subjectively why music or sound stirred him, why it advertised an unknown life of which no man ever told:

The field of my life becomes a boundless plain, glorious its tread, with no death or disappointment at the end of it. All meanness and trivialness disappear. I become adequate to any deed. No particulars survive this expansion; persons do not survive it. In the light of this strain there is no thou or I. We are actually lifted above ourselves.

This passage reflects pure mysticism; it is very close to Brahmanic *Anand*. This remarkable passage mirrors *Anand* in three ways: First, delight in existence which is a capacity to receive things in a spirit of equanimity. Second, all consciousness of duality vanishes—the "I am" ceases to exist in the affirmation of the "I am" in the "Thou art." Third, the role of action which reveals *Anand* or delight of existence is action in the spirit of sacrifice or an act of self-giving for the sake of the divine. Although this aspect of *Anand* is not stated specifically in Thoreau's analysis, the passage as a whole has a self-giving case. Thoreau expressed his joy in existence thus, "I thank you, God. I do not deserve anything. I am not worthy of the least regard, and yet I am made to rejoice."

Thoreau's analysis of the effect of *music* exhibits great profundity and is similar to Brahmanic *Anand;* it has a true ring of delight in existence, a fulfillment of being in the awareness that the meaning of life was discoverable in the principle behind creation. As he wrote in the *Week:*

> These simple sounds relate us to the star . . . How can I go on . . . Suddenly Old Time winked at me . . . Ah, you know me, you rogue . . . and news has come that it was well. That ancient universe is in such capital health, I think undoubtedly it will never die. Heal yourselves, doctors, by God I live.

Compare this with Rabindranath's assertion:

> Gladness is the one criterion of truth as we know when we have touched Truth by the music it gives, by the joy of the greeting it sends forth in us. That is the true foundation of all religions.

In order to show that Thoreau's ideas of universal rhythm were not unique in the extreme, one may quote from Sri Aurobindo in *The Life Divine:* "The worlds beyond exist: they have their universal rhythm, their grand lines and foundations, their self-existent laws and mighty energies—their just and luminous means of knowledge."

Henry Thoreau was cognizant not only of the need to surrender his individual self to the Universal self, but, more important, of the great individual effort required to effect mystical union. As he noted: "There is something proudly thrilling in the thought that this obedience to conscience and trust in God, which is so solemnly preached in extremities and arduous circumstances is only to retreat into oneself, and rely on our own strength." And he added that he could not afford to relax discipline because God was on his side for "He is on the side of discipline." He was fully alive to the fact that to know and to love God necessitates a course of action that is difficult to the extreme. Thoreau defined the intricate "mystic way"—the ethical strenuousness, the life of spiritual discipline and purity—which are the conditions so necessary for the final mystical union with God. Thoreau was persistent in striving to efface the multiplicity of the world in order to reach a state of absolute purity and simplicity.

In all mysticism there is a recognition of a basic dualism in man—the dichotomy existing in the soul of man which creates two distant sets of values that are at cross-purposes: *To be* versus *To have; the perfection of man* versus *the perfection of things.* *To be* denotes the perfection of man, spiritual realization and eternity; *To have* denotes perfection of things and material realization. The mystic not only recognizes these irreconcilable values, but is determined that negative values must be effaced through purgation. Just a few years before his death, Thoreau wrote in his journal that a man who had spent his time in business and who had acquired "much money, many houses, and barns and woodlots" surely had been a failure in life. He went even further and equated sin and death with material realization. Later his strictures became even more severe when he declared that simple acts are poetic, but trade is not simple but "artificial and complex." And not only does it postpone life but actually substitutes death. Rabindranath Tagore writes in the same vein when he says: "For those among whom the spiritual sense is dull, the desire for realization is reduced to physical possession, a dull grasping in space."

Thoreau believed that the essential object of man in

life was the constant aspiration for perfection. But in order to aspire to inspiration, there must first be expiration or purgation of being. To live, according to him, is to "let in the flood, raise the gates and set all our wheels in motion." After living for a few months at Walden Pond, Thoreau propounded his belief in a "hard and emphatic" life and his desire "to roam far, to grasp life and to conquer it, learn much and live." His ceaseless endeavor to reach the perfect and his realization, in fact, his obsession with the paradox that man is not what he is but something much greater is reflected in his exhortation: "Be resolutely and faithfully what you are: be humbly what you aspire to be."

Thoreau's basic concept of man was in harmony with all religions and all mystics. Sri Aurobindo states this clearly in *The Life Divine* when he declares that the quality and purpose of individual perfection are the divine life. "A spiritual fulfillment of the urge to individual perfection and an inner completeness of being." Rabindranath Tagore says in a similar vein: "Religion consists in the endeavour of man to cultivate and express those qualities which are inherent in the nature of Man the Eternal and to have faith in him."

We may now consider another essential aspect of mysticism: meditation or contemplation, one of the last steps up the mystical ladder to Being and one found in all mystical traditions. This aspect of mysticism can be called spiritual concentration. In the contemplative state, one finds the progressive surrender of self Lord. The mystic must efface all worldliness, wilfulness, and sense perception— only then will the Word be spoken. The *Bhagavad Gita* says, "Let the Yogi try constantly to concentrate his mind on the Superior Self, remaining in solitude and alone, self-controlled, free from desire and longings for possessions." The great Hindu scriptures, *Vedas, Upanishads,* and *Gita,* were written thousands of years ago by holy men who retired to forests to contemplate the very nature of self. Another passage from the *Katha Upanishad* concerning the contemplative state is as follows:

> His form is not an object of vision, no one beholds Him with the eye. One can know Him when He is revealed by the intellect free from doubt and by constant meditation. Those who know this become immortal.

Thoreau's understanding of contemplation is closely related to these words. In the context of this statement from the *Katha Upanishad,* Atman or the Supreme Soul is entirely imperceptible. Through meditation or right understanding, Brahma or Atma is revealed, not as an object but as the Supreme unity.

Sri Aurobindo also stresses the vital importance of the inner life of meditation and contemplation when he states that the liberation of self is impossible without "inward living." The Indian poet and mystic Kabir wrote: "By saying that Supreme Reality only dwells in the inner realms of spirit, we share the outer world of matter."

Both Indian mystics illustrate an important consideration that there are in the contemplative state two distinctive types of mystic awareness. One of these types is the mysticism of unifying vision—called extrovertive mysticism by Walter Stace. This is implied in the previous citations from the *Katha Upanishad,* as well as from Kabir, Aurobindo, and Tagore. The other type is the mysticism of introspection, so called by Stace; here there is a withdrawal from the multiplicity of the world into the core of the soul.

What was Thoreau's apparent understanding and practice of contemplation? Curiously enough, one does find both the unifying vision and introspectiveness in his experience. If Thoreau wished to be pure always, it was only to enable him to be at the top of his conditions, ready for whatever turned up in heaven or earth. He wanted to be in "right knowledge" so that he could commune with the Supreme Unity of the Cosmos. In *Bhagavad Gita* he apparently found the answer to some of the knotty questions that arise from the dedication to being through contemplation. There he found the manifest problem of a life of action and inaction, the active life and the contemplative life.

"What is action? What is inaction? Even the wise are puzzled by this question," Sri Krishna tells the warrior Arjuna in the *Bhagavad Gita*.

The answer that Thoreau probably read in this work was that both lead to enlightenment, although by different paths. "For the contemplative is the path of knowledge; for the active is the path of selfless action." The "pure intellectuality" of this answer appealed to Thoreau. He discovered that the sublime conservatism of these laws was congenial to his own nature and temperament, but the final goal of the enlightened state was even more pleasing. "The end is an immense consolation," he wrote in the *Week*, "eternal absorption in Brahma."

What appealed to him above all was the Hindu concept of inaction or the contemplative life. How long have those "Eastern sages sat contemplating Brahma, uttering in silence the mystic 'Om,' being absorbed into the essence of the Supreme Being," he wrote ecstatically in the *Week*.

Thoreau not only appreciated the "wonderful peace of abstraction" but stressed for his Yankee readers their "moral grandeur and sublimity." Thoreau spoke of the "wonderful retirement through which he moved," and thought this type of life was a practice of yoga. "Depend upon it that rude and careless as I am, I would fain practice the *yoga* faithfully." With this profession one finds irrefutable evidence that Thoreau's main life view was to attain being or *to be*, for mystical union is the desire for being or *to be*. Tagore says in a similar vein: "Mystical union has its significance not in the realm of *to have*, but in that of *to be*."

Thoreau affirmed to Harrison Blake that "to some extent and at rare intervals even I am a *yogi*." How highly Thoreau cherished the inactive life of the yoga, the contemplative life in solitude, can be illustrated by the fact that he devoted two complete chapters of *Walden* and parts of several others not only to extol the positive virtues of solitude and the meditative life in general, but to show in particular how he himself was a devotee of the yoga while at Walden Pond.

In his love for, in fact his absolute need for, solitude, Thoreau was simply affirming a basic doctrine of all mysticism. The vital need of the mystic for solitude is obvious: first, the need for intensification and amplification of purity and simplicity; second, there is need for the conditions favorable to meditator and contemplation. In the "stillness and solitude" of nature, Thoreau says he felt as if he had come to an open window; as he put it, "I see out and around myself." Rabindranath Tagore, whose life view is remarkably similar to Thoreau's, describes the same general experience in the following manner:

> In our soul we are conscious of the transcendent truth in us: the Universal, the Supreme Man; and this soul, the spiritual self has its enjoyment in the renunciation of the individual self for the sake of supreme soul.

Thoreau's propensity for the pure and simple life was matched only by his ardor for the solitary life. "I will build my lodge on the southern slope of some hill and take there the life the gods send me." These may be compared to the lines in the *Bhagavad Gita:*

> Let the *yogi* try constantly to concentrate his mind on the Supreme Self, remaining in solitude and alone, self-controlled, free from desires and longing for possessions.

Like the yogis of ancient India, like the mystics of East and West, Thoreau was a man of one idea, and that idea was the attainment of mystical union with God. In essence, the infinite in him, his core of light, sought the perfect knowledge of love rather than being attached to temporal things; he had an awareness of self rather than having self-love. He possessed humility, an integral part of mystical purity and simplicity. Like the Rishis of old he built his dwelling by the edge of water, a pond. Like Rabindranath Tagore he preferred the sylvan surroundings of nature; like Mahatma Gandhi he chose to live in a simple hut made by his own hands.

Henry Thoreau's mystical thoughts, practices, and ultimate conclusions, which have been briefly analysed in this address, are most strikingly in accord with those of the great mystics. His life and writings reveal a remarkable affinity with Indian thought. Thoreau appropriately concluded by affirming that "John or Jonathan" may not realize the resurrection or immortality of the soul, but the eternal "Now," the moment when time and eternity met, was still the character of each day.

Walden ends in this passage:

> The light which puts out our eyes is darkness to us, only that day dawns to which we are awake. There is more day to dawn. The sun is but a morning star.

It seems most significant that he closes this book with such lines, for the *Bhagavad Gita* phrases the same idea in this manner:

> What is night for all beings is the time for the waking of the disciplined soul; and what is the time of waking for all is the night for the seer who sees.

However, Thoreau influenced Indian thought in the twentieth century in a dramatic and most significant manner. His pamphlet on "Civil Disobedience," written primarily to oppose the payment of taxes to his government, affected Mahatma Gandhi's thinking greatly. Little did Thoreau foresee that his pamphlet would become the basis for the forging of a political weapon, "Satyagraha," powerful enough, in the hands of Mahatma Gandhi, to shake the very foundations of the British Empire in India. "Civil Disobedience" brought freedom to the Indian nation.

The Thoreau–Gandhi Syndrome

Nissim Ezekiel

IT IS PLEASANT FOR AN INDIAN TO ATTEND A THOREAU FESTI-
val in America and to speak about Thoreau's influence on
Gandhi. But the situation has its dangers. It is easy to
praise Thoreau, to praise Gandhi, and then to prove that
the one influenced the other. An American audience
would, of course, love such a story, and the Indian who
tells it is likely to be popular. The festival spirit is sus-
tained; a reason is found for self-congratulation; and everybody is then free to live as he pleases, without reference
to Thoreau or Gandhi.

I know that in the audience are authorities on Thoreau.
There are also some familiar with the life and ideas of
Gandhi. But perhaps not many are well acquainted with
both Thoreau and Gandhi. So I am in the enviable position of getting away with whatever assertions I choose to
make concerning the relation of Gandhian thought to
Thoreau. In certain circumstances, of which the present
is an example, an Indian or an American is naturally
tempted to exaggerate in the interests of what he considers
to be harmonious international relations in general and
comforting Indo-American relations in particular.

I would like to give two instances of such exaggeration,
not to blame these particular authors but to correct a
widespread belief. In 1932 Frederick B. Fisher published
a book with the interesting title, *That Strange Little*

Brown Man Gandhi (New York: Ray Long and Richard
R. Smith Inc.). Referring to Gandhi's persistent attachment to Thoreau's essay on civil disobedience, he writes,
"A curious friendship, this, of ancient India for young
America, still in its national swaddling clothes in the family of the ages! Yet the Indian peaceful revolution has
taken many of its weapons from the minds and lips of
Americans. In a very real sense the seeds of Indian revolution were planted in America." This I consider to be mis-
leading and sentimental, a very partial truth which has
become distorted in the defining.

It happened to be in the same year that an Indian writer
published in New York *Gandhi Versus the Empire,* with a
foreword by Will Durant (New York: Universal Publishing Co.). This author told his American readers defini-
tively that "his [Thoreau's] teachings are today the main-
spring of the Indian Non-violent Revolution." He added
the following highly rhetorical words of misinformation
and gratuitous advice:

> Henry David Thoreau is known to the American people as
> the author of *Walden.* To Gandhi and India he is known pri-
> marily as the author of the immortal essay on *Civil Dis-
> obedience.* Yes, America, through Washington and Lincoln,
> and especially through Thoreau, may be held responsible for
> the motif of the present non-violent revolution in India.
> Gandhi is today giving back to America what he received
> from her by way of Thoreau. The American people can best
> show their esteem for Gandhi by enshrining Thoreau in their
> hearts.

This was part of an attempt by Indian nationalists to
interest Americans in Gandhi and the movement for national independence. The appeal to Thoreau's influence
was calculated to establish a link which in reality is a rather
tenuous one. Even if, as the Indian writer suggests so
quaintly, Americans enshrine Thoreau in their hearts,
they may find Gandhi an altogether different proposition.

Thoreau is relatively simple and self-consistent. Gandhi is complex, ambiguous, comprehensively radical or revolutionary, thoroughgoing in his absolutes, yet full of intensely personal compromises and contradictions. Though there are a few affinities between the two men, the differences in their ideas and ways of living are deep and extensive.

Thoreau was a recluse even outside the period of the Walden experiment, which lasted only two years. Gandhi, a leader of groups and mass movements, was rarely alone. Thoreau never married and had little to say about sex. Gandhi was married as an adolescent to a child bride and had four children, but lived as a celibate from the age of thirty and spoke and wrote endlessly about sex and sexual problems. Thoreau avoided the church. Gandhi was his own church and conducted a mass prayer meeting every evening of his life. Thoreau loved nature. Gandhi was indifferent to it. Thoreau spent twenty-four hours in jail as a symbolic protest. Gandhi spent many years in jail, repeatedly courting it to assert the authority of the individual moral conscience against injustice. Thoreau sought and found a harmony between himself and his natural environment. Gandhi suffered agonies of the spirit throughout his life, and exalted suffering into a major part of his creed, as well as of his method of persuading and converting his opponents.

Both Thoreau and Gandhi were vegetarians and abstained from liquor, but only Gandhi fought all his life for prohibition as a national and international policy, for vegetarianism as an indispensable basis for the moral life. Recognition of these attitudes leads an American admirer of Gandhi, Homer A. Jack, to write rather wistfully: "Some of Gandhi's prescriptions were somewhat provincial in that they were not completely relevant to other cultures" (*The Gandhi Reader*, ed. Homer A. Jack. Bloomington: Indiana University Press, 1956). Very few students of Gandhian ideology are willing to confront the startling fact that for Gandhi sex—except for the purpose of having children—was against the laws of God and man. When someone pointed out that this would imply very few sexual meetings for most couples throughout their marriage, Gandhi remarked that a few times are enough. There is nothing in Thoreau's writings to compare with such formidable absolutism, on sex or on any other subject. It is this element of Gandhism which makes the British political and social critic George Orwell call it "inhuman," though he pays Gandhi the tribute of saying that he "enriched the world simply by being alive" ("Reflections on Gandhi" in the *Orwell Reader,* ed. Richard Rovere. New York: Harcourt, Brace, 1959).

It is in trying to find out what such a tribute means in relation to Gandhi and Thoreau that one discovers the precise scope of the influence. If we read Gandhi's autobiography, we come to realize that the seeds of the Indian non-violent revolution were not planted in America but belong to the Indian ethical and spiritual tradition. When Thoreau wrote that "the pure Walden water is mingled with the sacred water of the Ganges," he was acknowledging his debt to that tradition. Gandhi's struggle as a child and adolescent to establish truth-telling as the moral basis of his life was instinctively of the Indian moral tradition as expressed through the influence of his mother. When he deviated from it, the timely reading of a literary or religious classic brought him back, not converted, but saved and confirmed.

Henry Salt's *Plea for Vegetarianism* did not make him a vegetarian: he was one from birth. It enabled him to avoid further guilty experiments in meat-eating. "My young mind," Gandhi writes in his *Autobiography,* "tried to unify the teaching of the *Gita,* the *Light of Asia* by Sir Edwin Arnold and the Sermon on the Mount." These early influences were unified after experiments in Westernization which not only failed miserably and ridiculously, but which also recalled him to his true soul and to the true soul of India as he experienced it. Thomas Merton, in the introduction to his selections from Gandhi on nonviolence, identifies this as the first and greatest of revolutions in the mind of Gandhi, the one from which the others flowed. At that time, it should be remembered, Gandhi had heard of neither Thoreau nor Tolstoy.

Gandhi arrived at the first phase of his spiritual journey not by doing the right thing, but by doing the wrong thing with every ounce of his earnestness. He set out, while studying for the Matriculation in London, to accomplish "the all-too-impossible task," as he put it, "of becoming an English gentleman." After all, he had defied his caste in going abroad and the community had excommunicated him, made him an outcast. He bought expensive English clothes in the latest fashion of the time, discarding the not-so-fashionable English clothes which had been made for him by a tailor in Bombay. He added an evening suit to his wardrobe and went in for a chimney-pot hat. He learned to wear a tie. At his request, his brother sent him a double watch chain of gold from India. Inquiring as to the means of becoming an Englishman, he was advised to "take lessons in dancing, French and elocution." Six lessons in ballroom dancing led to the realization that he had no ear for Western music. He decided to cultivate it by learning to play the violin; accordingly he bought an instrument and engaged a tutor. Thus we envision Gandhi at twenty, in London, in the year 1888, practicing ballroom dancing, learning to play the violin, studying French, and finally taking a speech by William Pitt from Bell's *Standard Elocutionist* and reciting it over and over again.

At this point came the Great Awakening. The attempt at Westernization was given up, and Gandhi was reborn as an Indian, restored to his own heritage.

Thoreau comes into the picture in the early South African phase of Gandhi's life. He had gone there in 1893, at the age of twenty-four, merely to plead a legal case. But he soon became involved in the struggle of the local Indians against the harsh discriminatory practices of the white rulers. In addition to a courageous personal defiance of these, for which he paid in physical and mental suffering, Gandhi was evolving a mode of organized mass resistance to them. He had read Tolstoy's *The Kingdom of God is Within You,* which had "overwhelmed" him and left "an abiding impression." The idea of soul force, or moral force, was encouraged by this experience. Ruskin's *Unto This Last* helped to fill out a new vision of social and economic relations in conformity with the basic principles of a traditional Indian culture as Gandhi saw it.

Thoreau's "Civil Disobedience" came into Gandhi's hands at this point. I shall quote two authorities on Gandhi: the first documents the facts of the event and the influence as vouched for by an associate of Gandhi; the second establishes the proper time sequence. H. S. L. Polak reports that the Thoreau pamphlet arrived at a "critical moment" and encouraged Gandhi in conducting his programme of passive resistance:

> His [Thoreau's] argument that a man must obey his own conscience even against the will of his fellow-citizens and be ready to undergo imprisonment in consequence—for, after all, it was only his body and not his spirit which was in custody—appealed strongly to Mahatma Gandhi. He pressed me to publish it as a supplement to *Indian Opinion* (Appendix in *Tolstoy and Gandhi* by Kalidas Nag. Patna: Pustak Bhander, 1950).

The other quotation is from a study by Gopinath Dhawan, *The Political Philosophy of Mahatma Gandhi* (Bombay: Popular Book Depot, 1946):

> Gandhiji however did not derive his idea of Civil Disobedience from the writings of Thoreau. The resistance to

authority in South Africa was well advanced before he got
the essay of Thoreau. . . . The movement was then known
as Passive Resistance. Gandhiji began to use Thoreau's phrase
to explain the struggle to the English readers, but he found
that even "Civil Disobedience" failed to convey the full
meaning of the struggle. So he adopted the phrase "Civil
Resistance."

In later years all these phrases were freely used by
Gandhi and his followers to describe any Gandhian fight
against injustice, which was essentially based on nonviolence, or *ahimsa*. The word Gandhi used most frequently
to describe such a struggle was one coined in South Africa:
Satyagraha, or Truth-force. The struggle derived one of
its earliest inspirations from Thoreau's idea that the authority of those in power is largely based on its acceptance
by the people: it is moral, not physical. Resistance to that
authority, therefore, should rely on moral force. From
this synthesis Gandhi proceeded to elaborate a technique
of mass struggle and what he called a Constructive Programme, which involved voluntary, dedicated service to
humanity without any expectation of rewards or even results. All this was well beyond anything envisaged by
Thoreau. In fact, even when Gandhi quotes Thoreau he
carries the ideas forward in a direction and to a point that
Thoreau might well have found embarrassing.

An instructive example would be Thoreau's description
of his feelings during his twenty-four-hour imprisonment.
He contrasts his actual feelings with those that are likely
to be attributed to him by people outside who think they
are free. "I did not feel for a moment confined," Thoreau
says. But he sees no reason to produce an elaborate apo-
logia for jail-going, which is exactly what Gandhi does.
Though he writes half-humorously, there is no denying
the very special attitude to life which is revealed in the
following remarks by Gandhi about prison:

There is very little of that misery which man has usually to undergo in daily life. [What misery? Thoreau would have asked in bewilderment.] There, he has to carry out the orders of one warder only, whereas in daily life he is obliged to carry out the behests of a great many more. [I carry out no man's behests, Thoreau might have commented.] In the jail, he has no anxiety to earn his daily bread and to prepare his meals. [Thoreau experienced no anxiety on this score, and of those who do, few would want to give it up for the dubious pleasures of life in jail.] It also looks after his health for which he has to pay nothing. He gets enough work to exercise his body. He is freed from all his vicious habits. [Again, a bewildered Thoreau would have asked, What vicious habits?] His soul is thus free. He has plenty of time at his disposal to pray to God.

I quote in this way, interrupting with comments, to emphasize what I regard as a special feature of Gandhian thought, which I have already mentioned: its exultation in suffering and its insistence on transforming suffering into joy. An extreme mystical strain in Gandhi enabled him not only to preach but successfully to practice this doctrine. For most of his followers, needless to say, it was not easy.

Gandhi was not in the habit of reading extensively. He reread a few scriptures (using the word both literally and metaphorically) over and over again, meditated on them unendingly, and drew from them an ever-renewed flow of inspiration. Thoreau's essay on civil disobedience was undoubtedly one of these scriptures, though there is no evidence that Gandhi ever read *Walden* or any other of Thoreau's writings. Twenty-five years or so after he had first read it, on the occasion of one of his arrests in Bombay, a copy of "Civil Disobedience" was found by his bedside. And it is on record that he took it along with him to prison. We may be sure that he reread it then and repeatedly in the years that followed.

In 1930, Gandhi and the people of India faced a Press

Ordinance of the British government which required all journals and papers to deposit a security, to be forfeited if anything seditious was published. Gandhi surrendered the Navjivan Press, which had published his periodical *Young India,* rather than pay the security. The journal was thereafter mimeographed. In a public statement, Gandhi said:

> Let us realize the wise dictum of Thoreau that it is difficult, under tyrannical rule, for honest men to be wealthy, and if we have decided to hand over our bodies without murmur to the authorities, let us also be equally ready to hand over our property to them and not sell our souls.

It may be argued that such a surrender was poor tactics, but Gandhiji saw it in terms of the purity of suffering. If the object of a struggle is not to gain one's own ends but to convert the opponent by soul-force, such gestures are necessary. Gandhi believed that Thoreau and others like him had helped to abolish slavery by the force of their moral gestures. By refusing to pay taxes, Thoreau had not deprived his Government of much money, but he had set an example of noncooperation with violence and injustice.

Noncooperation, by many if possible, but even by only a few if necessary, became a central principle in Gandhi's creed. One honest Satyagrahi, Gandhi used to say, acting out of the strength of his faith, was more useful than hundreds who had no faith or who accepted the method because they had no alternative, no weapon. This is unquestionably an echo of Thoreau: "If one *honest* man in this state of Massachusetts were actually to withdraw from cooperating with the government and be locked up in the country jail, then it would be the abolition of slavery in America." What is common to Thoreau and Gandhi is faith in the moral power of the individual, particularly if expressed in specific actions dictated by the free expression of conscience.

Gandhi had made such gestures *before* he read Thoreau. They express the spirit of Gandhi, in my opinion, better than much of his doctrine. In London, when he was barely twenty years old, he asserted that spirit in a most striking way. He had joined the Vegetarian Society and had been elected to its Executive Committee. One of its members publicly advocated artificial methods of birth control, making many enemies. Gandhi agreed with the others in their opposition to birth control, but he felt that the question had nothing to do with vegetarianism. When the offending member found himself threatened with the prospect of not being reelected, Gandhi took his side. Eventually Gandhi resigned on the ground that the objections of the others to the birth control advocate's position were unconnected with the purposes of the Society. He put aside his own powerful prejudices—for he had a tremendous abhorrence of birth control—risked unpopularity, and finally separated himself from the cause which attracted him more than any other at that time.

Gandhi's vision of a free India has some affinities with Thoreau's view of society and government. He often quoted Thoreau's dictum, "That government is best which governs the least." But he went further than Thoreau in opposing the existence not only of the armed forces but also of the police. He wanted all organized control of social institutions to be decentralized to the stage where political power itself would be dissolved and the state with it. Human beings should change themselves, experience a change of heart, as Gandhi put it, to make themselves worthy of such a condition. He also insisted that good ends could never be attained by corrupt means. There is an elaborate Gandhian theory of conflict resolution. Thoreau confined his idea of civil disobedience to a form of protest. Gandhi wanted protest without any feeling of enmity, a superhuman demand. His noncooperation was as much in his opponents' interests as in his own. In politics,

Thoreau suggested a courageous defiance of authority wherever necessary, but in a simple, practical, idealistic manner. Gandhi stands for a saintly, religious self-purification in action through love of the enemy. These two positions should not be confused.

It should be clear that I am not praising Gandhi in comparison with Thoreau or expressing the view that because his position is apparently more exalted it is necessarily more true. As I said earlier, Gandhi is ambiguous and can be interpreted in different ways to support a variety of ideas. One Indian writer observes, "Gandhism in a way has become an ideological bank where different people can obtain support for their current needs" ("Gandhism Reexamined," Ashakant Nimbark in *Social Research* 31, no. 1, 1964). It is virtually impossible to treat Thoreau in this way, though attempts are sometimes made. President Sukarno of Indonesia, whose theory and practice were far removed from Gandhi and Thoreau, claimed—and with some justification—that he and the whole Afro-Asian movement were inspired by both. In Asia, Africa, and the United States (particularly in some aspects of the American Negro's struggle for equal rights), it is not the differences between Thoreau and Gandhi that are noticed, but the affinities. Some of Thoreau's ideas, inspired by Indian thought, influenced Gandhi, whose techniques of mass struggle have been found useful in other countries of Asia and Africa, and returned to America where they are now undergoing a new transformation. The life of Martin Luther King exemplifies this process, with a Christian orientation.

Thoreau's Influence on One Life

George Russell Ready

THE TONE OF MY DISCUSSION IS SET BY HENRY THOREAU. WHEN I first planned this short talk, I thought of doing something scholarly; but I think what I will do is to leave the scholarship to the scholars and take as my text a quotation from the first page of *Walden,* where Thoreau says, "Moreover, I, on my side, require of every writer, first or last, a simple and sincere account of his own life, and not merely what he has heard of other men's lives; some such account as he would send to his kindred from a distant land; for if he has lived sincerely it must have been in a distant land to me." I should add here that I also exercise Henry's preference for talking in the first person. So today, with your indulgence, I would like to tell you a little about myself and the influence of Thoreau in my life.

My first twenty years were spent on a small farm in Ontario, about thirty-five miles south of Ottawa. At that time, that would be forty-eight years ago, forty-nine this year, much of the territory around there was very like Concord, Massachusetts, the same kind of land roughly, and we experienced many of the natural phenomena that Thoreau so nicely described in his writings. In those days, my father had only fifty acres of land, not very much in the best of times, and we were also struggling through the

Great Depression. My father added to our meager income by doing handyman jobs like carpentry, plumbing, electrical work, anything to make a few dollars. Consequently, as I grew up, I developed, like Thoreau, as many trades as fingers.

I dropped out of high school in 1935, when I was seventeen. At the age of twenty, I went to work for the Bell Telephone Company of Canada in Montreal, and I stayed with Bell for twenty-seven years. (That, I think, is why I have these wrinkles.) In 1953, at the age of thirty-five, I went back to school in the evenings. In 1957 I was graduated as a Bachelor of Arts.

At present, I teach in the English Department of the Eastern Ontario Institute of Technology. Now, this organization is being united with other schools to form Algonquin College (I think Henry Thoreau might like our name, Algonquin, a fine Indian name.)

I really cannot remember my first conscious exposure to Henry Thoreau. I was quite a reader in my childhood, and I remember, as I search through my mind, having read somewhere "The Battle of the Ants." That impressed me; and I have never forgotten it. I remember that a little later I read an article concerning the fact that so many of our artists have died young. The author cited Stevenson, Keats, Chopin, and also Henry Thoreau.

My overwhelming conversion to Thoreauvian thought dates from 1939, during my first summer in Montreal. I had bought a copy of *Walden* to while away the hours in Montreal streetcars. The reason I had bought it in the first place was that the blurb on the back cover described it as the story of a man who believed in doing what he wanted, my own philosophy of living. I read *Walden* three times in succession. Since that time it has been my *vade mecum*. It has never been very far from me. Thoreau said, "I have lived some thirty years on this planet, and I have yet to hear the first syllable of valuable or even earnest advice from my seniors." But my experience with Thoreau himself makes it necessary for me to disagree with him, something I seldom do, for I owe so much to his conscious and unconscious prodding, I am certain that, without the discovery of his writings, my life would be spectacularly different. In other words, often said before, once a man has read *Walden* he will never be the same again.

Why? The best answer would probably be to read you the whole of *Walden*. But failing that, I'd like to look at four key quotations. Thoreau says, "I do not speak to those who are well-employed in whatever circumstances, and they know whether they are well-employed or not— but mainly to the mass of men who are discouraged and idly complaining of the hardness of their lot or their times, when they might improve them."

He adds, "Perhaps these pages are more particularly addressed to poor students" (and aren't we all poor students) ; "as for the rest of my readers, they will accept such portions as apply to them. I trust that none will stretch the seams in putting on the coat, for it may do good service to him whom it fits."

And then the third one, "I would not have anyone adopt *my* mode of living on any account; for, besides that before he has fairly learned it I may have found out another for myself, I desire that there be as many different persons in the world as possible, but I would have each one be very careful to find out and pursue *his own* way, and not his father's or his mother's or his neighbor's instead."

Finally, "men do not fail for lack of knowledge, but for lack of prudence to give wisdom the preference."

When one reads even these few quotations, he marvels at the things that Henry Thoreau knew without having had to learn them. No one has, I think, compressed in a short sentence Thoreau's genius so well as our friend

Theodore Dreiser when he said that it is as if "some god alive at the beginning of the world should break through in Thoreau and remember something of what nature's mind is." There is some great magic about *Walden*, of course, and *Walden* exudes some kind of universal solvent that pervades the tissues of some fortunate individuals, never to be completely dissipated.

I was one of those fortunate individuals. During my twenty-seven years at the Telephone Company, I was moderately successful. I was promoted in 1950 to a supervisory position, and from that time on until I left the Bell, I was concerned with management and technical training; but all the time in the back of my mind, what I had learned from Thoreau remained dormant, in a sense.

As years passed I suddenly discovered that I was becoming a senior citizen in the Telephone Company and that other fellows were passing me by, and that set my nose out of joint. Especially today there is a trend in large corporations to select the "jet" supervisors—young fellows who are chosen for their ability to apply pressure. (A Thoreauvian tends, I think, to be not a soft individual, certainly, but perhaps more placid and more understanding.) Then, at my yearly medical examination, we found that my blood pressure was going up two points a year. I went to the doctor, who said that a trip to the Mayo Clinic should possibly be my next move.

At this point the earlier inoculation of Thoreau took effect, and particularly this quotation: "Why should we be in such desperate haste to succeed and in such hurry and waste of life; we are determined to be starved before we are hungry; a stitch in time saves nine and we use one thousand stitches to save nine tomorrow."

Now, think of working for a communications company and having these things banging in the back of your head! "Why should we be in such desperate haste to succeed and in such desperate enterprises? If a man does not keep pace with his companions, perhaps it is because he hears a different drummer. Let him step to the music which he hears, however measured or far away." And, "What are three score years and ten lived hurriedly and coarsely to moments of divine leisure in which your life is coincident with the life of the universe. We live too fast and coarsely just as we eat too fast and do not know the true savor of food." So, if things were going to continue in the same way, I thought, I would not reach my three score years and ten.

And then one of those telling blows at pension plans: "The spending of the best part of one's life earning money in order to enjoy a questionable liberty during the least valuable part of it." That should be written on everyone's hat band. We should read that every day. Thoreau is like the Bible. You can go in anywhere you want and get a nudge in the right place: "Making yourself sick that you may lay up something against a sick day, something to be tucked away in an old chest or in a sock behind the plastering, or more safely in a brick bank, no matter where, no matter how." And then this very, very demolishing comment: "The cost of a thing is the amount of what I call life which is required to be exchanged for it immediately or in the long run." And "Superfluous wealth can buy superfluities only. Money is not required to buy one necessity for the soul."

We know that Thoreau was a severe social critic, but he puts matters in perspective, for me anyway, when he says, "no matter how mean your life is, meet it and live it; do not shun it and call it hard names. It is not so bad as you are. It looks poorest when you are richest. The fault-finder will find faults even in paradise." Then also the quotation where he asks us to decide if we should live like men or baboons. Isn't that a question!

With Thoreau's words in mind, then, I was able to

leave the telephone company at the age of forty-seven, and I moved into teaching just as if I had stepped out of the shadow and into the sunlight.

I never would have believed, say, fifteen years earlier, that I *could do that;* but as you know, Henry said so many things about this—"the sun rises fresh every morning" and "we do not really know our capabilities," and the like.

I am thankful to Henry Thoreau who convinced me that I should cultivate my five cubic feet of flesh. I'm far from cultivated yet, but Henry showed the way.

I would like to close with Thoreau's admonition, "Be it life or death, we crave only reality. If we are really dying, let us hear the rattle in our throats and feel cold in the extremities; if we are alive, let us go about our business."

Walking Westward

Jack Schwartzman

AS CO-HOST AND LAST SPEAKER AT THE THOREAU FESTIVAL, I stand before this assembly in order to bid farewell to its many distinguished guests—many of them my friends of long standing—and to attempt to summarize, in a brief address, the spirit and the dream that was Henry David Thoreau.

It is perhaps fitting that my talk is based on the two essays written by Thoreau in the last year of his life, when he was about ready to "walk westward." In 1862, shortly before his death, he completed "Walking" and "Wild Apples." (It is ironic that my talk on walking is delivered to a *sitting* audience. However, it is appropriate that such a talk is delivered at the close of day, for the mystic concept of "walking" encompasses the inevitable—to Thoreau—direction of "westwardness.")

Professor Nissim Ezekiel, our worthy representative of the East, who just completed an eloquent address, undoubtedly knows what East and West meant to the Yankee sage. "We go eastward," said Thoreau, "to realize history and study the works of art and literature, retracing the steps of the race; we go westward as into the future, with a spirit of enterprise and adventure." To Thoreau, West is liberty. "Eastward," he stated, "I do only by force; but westward I go free."

"Take almost any path you please," declared Melville

150

in *Moby Dick,* "and ten to one it carries you down in a dale, and leaves you there by a pool in the stream. There is magic in it. Let the most absent-minded of men be plunged in his deepest reveries—stand that man on his legs, set his feet a-going, and he will infallibly lead you to water. . . . Yes, as every one knows, meditation and water are wedded for ever."

Contrast the above statement with the one made by Thoreau. "When I go out of the house for a walk," he wrote, "uncertain as yet whither I will bend my steps, and submit myself to my instinct to decide for me, I find, strange and whimsical as it may seem, that I finally and inevitably settle southwest. . . . My needle is slow to settle . . . but it always settles between west and south-southwest. The future lies that way to me, and the earth seems more unexhausted and richer on that side."

"Wildness," said Thoreau, "is the preservation of the world." To him, walking is marching with a purpose— and always in the direction of the West—for *there* lies wildness: wonderful, free, natural, exciting wildness. The degeneracy of man is in his *tameness,* his *dullness.* "It is hard for me to believe," Thoreau mused, "that I shall find fair landscapes or sufficient wildness and freedom behind the eastern horizon. I am not excited by the prospect of a walk thither; but I believe that the forest which I see in the western horizon stretches uninterruptedly toward the setting sun, and there are no towns nor cities in it of enough consequence to disturb me. Let me live where I will, on this side is the city, on that the wilderness, and ever I am leaving the city more and more, and withdrawing into the wilderness."

Thoreau's remarks were always addressed to Man the Individualist—not to man the citizen. "I wish to speak a word for Nature, for absolute freedom and wildness, as contrasted with a freedom and culture merely civil,—to regard man as an inhabitant, or a part or parcel of Nature,

rather than a member of society." Only the Individualist,
emphasized the one-time resident of Walden, can understand the feeling of walking, the taste of wild apples, the
magnetism of the West, and the intoxication of wildness.
Not for the pale-faced denizens of the ant-hills is meant
Thoreau's heady stimulant. He had nothing but contempt
for the "champions of civilization: the minister and the
school committee . . ." and all other conformist non-souls.

And speaking of wild apples: they are the symbol of
man's fierce, sharp, tangy, indomitable independence. "I
would have my thoughts, like wild apples," he exulted,
"to be food for walkers, and will not warrant them to be
palatable if tasted in the house. . . . I fear that he who
walks over these fields a century hence will not know the
pleasure of knocking off wild apples. Ah, poor man, there
are many pleasures which he will not know."

As a man walks westward, he walks as a free man. And
only in America, stated Thoreau, can a man walk freely
and "westwardly." "As a true patriot," he stated, "I should
be ashamed to think that Adam in paradise was more
favorably situated on the whole than the backwoodsman
in this country." (Compare this statement with the cele-
brated utterance of Thomas Paine: "The world is my
country, all mankind are my brethren, and to do good is
my religion.")

Walking, to Thoreau, is not just a routine, indifferent
exertion. It is a mystic rite: it is a godlike performance.
Listen to Thoreau's rapture: "I have met with but one
or two persons in the course of my life who understood
the art of Walking . . . our expeditions are but tours, and
come round again at evening to the old hearthside from
which we set out. Half the walk is but retracing our
steps. . . . If you are ready to leave father and mother,
and brother and sister, and wife and child and friends,
and never see them again—if you have paid your debts,

and made your will and settled all your affairs, and are a free man, then you are ready for a walk."

Not for the tame, dull, civilized, conforming "dead souls" is the sacred art of walking. And only those who are privileged to walk are able to trace their steps westward. And only those who are able to walk westward are able to achieve the joy of eating wild apples. And only those who taste the indescribable tanginess of wild apples are able to experience the ecstasy of wildness. And only those who experience the ecstasy of wildness are truly able to exist. They alone know the purpose of life: only to them do the gods of Nature speak a language that the plodding masses do not even hear. Only the select few are "right," in the absolute sense of the word. "Any man more right than his neighbors constitutes a majority of one."

We are bidding farewell to the great mystic of Concord. Let us, therefore, heed his wise farewell to us:

"So we saunter toward the Holy Land, till one day the sun shall shine more brightly than ever he has done, shall perchance shine into our minds and hearts, and light up our whole lives with a great awakening light, as warm and serene and golden as on a bankside in autumn."

About the Contributors

Kamala Bhatia, grandniece of poet and seer Aurobindo Ghose, participated in Mahatma Gandhi's Satyagraha movement and has been associated with the Gandhi Peace Foundation, and the Indian Council of World Affairs. Until recently she was a Field Adviser to the Ministry of Education in India. She has served as a Visiting Professor at the State University College at Brockport.

George Brenner is a former Dean at Nassau Community College and is now Professor of English there. He has directed all of the college's literary festivals and has lectured widely on both American and British authors. He is also a Consultant to Long Island University.

Philip Corner holds a Master's degree from Columbia and studied piano with Mrs. Dorothy Taubman. In Paris he worked in the field of composition under the guidance of Messiaen. Mr. Corner is co-founder with Malcolm and James Tenney of the performance group called "Tone-Roads."

Paul A. Doyle, Professor of English at Nassau Community College, is author or editor of nine books, the most recent being *Sean O'Faolain: A Critical Study* and *A Concordance of the Collected Poems of James Joyce*.

Nissim Ezekiel, Vice Principal and Chairman of the Department of English at Mithibai College (Bombay), is editor of *Poetry India*. He has published five volumes of poems and has edited *Writing in India* and *An Emerson*

Reader. His first volume of poetry, called *A Time to Change,* was published in London in 1951.

Walter Harding, one of the world's preeminent Thoreau scholars, has written or edited eighteen books about Thoreau. Included among his publications are *A Thoreau Handbook, Thoreau: Man of Concord, The Variorum Walden,* and the monumental study, *The Days of Henry Thoreau.* Dr. Harding is presently University Professor at the State University of New York College at Geneseo.

Donald Harrington is the Senior Minister of the Community Church of New York and a lecturer and commentator on many crucial national issues. He has been active in the New York Liberal Party, the American Committee on Africa, and countless other organizations.

Alfred Kazin is one of the best known and highly regarded twentieth-century American literary critics. Among his many books are *On Native Grounds, A Walker in the City,* and *The Inmost Leaf.* He presently serves on the English faculty at the State University branch at Stony Brook.

Lewis Leary, for many years Professor of English and Chairman of the English Department at the Graduate School of Columbia University, is now William Rand Kenan, Jr. Professor of English at the University of North Carolina. He has written numerous books, including studies of Freneau and Whittier, has edited the indispensable *Articles on American Literature, 1900–1954,* and has surveyed Thoreau scholarship in Stovall's *Eight American Authors: A Review of Research and Criticism.*

Frederick T. McGill is Professor of English and Associate Dean at Rutgers College of Arts and Sciences in Newark. His most recently published book is a very favorably reviewed study of William Ellery Channing.

George Russell Ready is President of the Thoreau Society

and is a member of the English faculty at Algonquin College in Ottawa, Ontario.

Muriel Rukeyser has been called by the *Times Literary Supplement* "one of America's greatest living poets." Among her many books are *Theory of Flight, A Turning Wind, The Life of Poetry, Elegies,* and *Waterlily Fire.* She is a member of the faculty of Sarah Lawrence College.

Jack Schwartzman is one of the founders and Editor-in-Chief of *Fragments,* and is the author of *Rebels of Individualism* and many scholarly articles. He holds a Ph.D. from New York University and a J.S.D. degree from Brooklyn Law School. He is Associate Professor of English at Nassau Community College.

Ruth R. Wheeler is a charter member and former vice-president of the Thoreau Society and serves as its archivist. She is deeply versed in the life, history, and lore of Concord. Her husband, Caleb Wheeler, is one of the ninth generation to live on the same farm in Concord.